Dark Psychology 101

Learn The Secrets Of Covert Emotional Manipulation, Dark Persuasion, Undetected Mind Control, Mind Games, Deception, Hypnotism, Brainwashing And Other Tricks Of The Trade

Michael Pace

Copyright 2015 by Michael Pace.

Published by Make Profits Easy LLC

Profitsdaily123@aol.com

facebook.com/MakeProfitsEasy

Table of Contents

Introduction: Welcome To The World's Most Powerful Psychology Book 4

Chapter 1: Covert Emotional Manipulation 9

Chapter 2: Dark Persuasion 26

Chapter 3: Undetected Mind Control 42

Chapter 4: Mind Games 57

Chapter 5: Deception 77

Chapter 6: Hypnotism 96

Chapter 7: Brainwashing 116

Chapter 8: The Dark Triad 136

Chapter 9: Dark Psychological Seduction 157

Chapter 10: Case Studies 183

Conclusion: Light At The End Of The Tunnel? 238

Introduction: Welcome To The World's Most Powerful Psychology Book

What Is Dark Psychology?

They say that knowledge is power. Well, if knowledge is power, then having knowledge of human psychology is the equivalent of having super powers. Psychology, the understanding of the human mind and the way it works, is a topic central to the existence of mankind. Psychology underpins everything from advertising to finance, crime to religion, and love to hate. Someone who understands psychological principles holds the key to human influence, a key few other people possess.

Obtaining psychological knowledge is often a difficult task. Like all of mankind's most advanced secrets, psychological knowledge is buried deep within the pages of dense journals and kept out of the reach of the general public. To distill this powerful information into a useful form would require someone to delve through countless books and journals, attempting to separate the useful from the useless.

That very process has been completed! You are reading a cutting-edge distillation of some of the most powerful principles in the world of psychology. You don't need any special understanding to benefit from this book, just a willingness to learn, reflect, and apply your new knowledge.

The book you now possess offers an insight into a hidden world that few people know exists and even fewer understand. The world of "dark psychology." These are the principles and tactics used by the most powerful influencers the world has ever known. You have a ticket to explore some of human history's most devious minds and the diabolical ideas they devised.

Not only will you be offered insight into the principles underpinning what essentially amounts to psychological black magic, you will be shown the ways the principles are actually applied.

And that's not all. Real-life case studies are offered so you can understand these ideas by seeing clearly how they have been used throughout history.

Why You Need To Understand Dark Psychology

Dark psychology is at work in the world. You might not like this fact, but you can't change it. So you have a choice: either try to remain ignorant of something powerful and risk becoming its next victim, or take control of your situation and learn to protect yourself, and those you love, from people who would ruin you through their ruthless psychological exploitation.

Understanding dark psychology is not only a defensive measure. There are ideas and principles contained within the world of dark psychology that can help you get ahead in your personal and professional endeavors. No one is asking you to become a psychopath, but surely you could use a little more power in your day-to-day life.

With Great Power Comes Great Responsibility

How you use this book is up to you. It can be the most powerful defensive tome you've ever come across, or a weapon used to give you an advantage in life. The ideas and examples contained in these pages are simply tools. Use them to build whatever you desire.

This book is not for the faint of heart or the weak of mind. Once you have lifted the curtain on the world of dark psychology, there is no going back. You will have an understanding of human nature

Covert refers to the way some manipulators are able to hide their intentions and the true nature of their actions. Not all emotional manipulation and influence can be categorized as covert. Victims of the covert type, however, will typically not know they have been manipulated, not understand the way manipulation has been carried out, and not even be able to guess at the motivation of their manipulator. CEM is a dark psychological stealth bomber, avoiding detection and defense until it is too late.

The emotional side of the manipulation refers to the specific focus of the manipulator. Other types of possible manipulation include people's behaviors, beliefs and willpower. CEM focuses specifically on impacting a person's emotional state and reality. Many manipulators focus in on this area of influence as they know a person's emotions are the key to all other aspects of their personality. Manipulating someone's emotions is like slicing their jugular vein. If a person has emotional control, they have full control.

The final piece of this puzzle is the term "manipulation." It is a common misunderstanding that influence and manipulation are the same thing. This is not the case. Manipulation refers to the underhand and hidden process of influence that takes place outside the awareness of the person being controlled. The intention behind influencing someone as opposed to the intention behind manipulating them is another key difference.

An influencer has the mindset of "I would like to help you make decisions that are good for you." A manipulator has the mentality of "I want to secretly control you to benefit myself." Therefore, understanding the intention behind any given behavior is in large part deciding whether it is an example of covert emotional manipulation or not.

Now you have an overview of exactly what covert emotional manipulation is and how it differs from other forms of influence and control. The most likely situations to find covert emotional manipulation taking place will now be explored as well as the main types of manipulative characters that occur time and time again.

Situations and Manipulators

Broadly speaking, there are four primary scenarios in which covert emotional manipulation can take place. These are the professional, personal, romantic, and family spheres of life. Romantic covert emotional manipulation is perhaps the most common scenario and can also be the most deadly. Less obvious forms of CEM can be found almost anywhere though. Once you understand the concept, and the practical applications of it, you will be able to guard against it, no matter what situation you find yourself in.

Just as there are common scenarios in which covert emotional manipulation can occur, there are common types of people who manifest the ideas underpinning CEM. Being able to link the theory of CEM to actual, personal portrayals of its ideas is an essential aspect of understanding it fully.

A controlling romantic partner is a common personal portrayal of the principles of CEM. If someone is in a relationship, and their partner is obviously trying to control them, the person is likely to be disgusted by what is happening and is looking to find a way out of the situation. For this reason, many controlling partners exercise their influence in the most covert way possible. Their girlfriend or wife ends up being a victim to total emotional manipulation without ever realizing it is taking place. This grants the manipulator the control they desire without any of the risks of being discovered and losing the other person for good.

A so-called "friend" might also make use of CEM to get the outcome they want out of their relationship with another person. In this specific group, one of the most common types of manipulator is someone who covertly induces in a friend the feelings of guilt, sympathy, and obligation toward them. The friend who is being manipulated in this way will be unaware that they are being influenced. They will not be able to explain why they feel and behave the way they do toward their "friend," the manipulator.

The professional domain is another common playground for covert emotional manipulators. Countless people have stories of having worked for a boss, or other person of authority, who seemed to trigger mysterious feelings of guilt, fear, or duty in them. People who have been manipulated in this way could never identify why these feelings exist or where they come from.

Family contexts are some of the most problematic within the world of CEM. A skilled manipulator who is able to find a victim within their own family is likely to be very dangerous in terms of the influence they can exercise. This is due to the fact that CEM is a powerful technique even when the manipulator and victim have no genuinely deep connection to each other. When the genuine connection of blood relation is added into the mix, the level of control and influence can increase exponentially.

Why are family situations so suited to the use of CEM? Simply put, people already feel a level of social obligation to help people out in their own family and "go the extra mile" to ensure their needs are attended to. This existing predisposition toward influence is added to by the covert emotional manipulative practices and the outcome is a very malleable victim.

So how exactly do covert emotional manipulators manage to instill such levels of control over their victims? They have a range of tactics that are hard to detect and even harder to resist. Read on to discover the secrets of the covert emotional manipulators.

Covert Manipulation Methods

You now know exactly what covert emotional manipulation is, and is not, and the types of situations it can occur in. This is a good foundational understanding of the topic, but it is also important to recognize some of the specific tactics used by manipulators in their pursuit of control. The entire purpose of this type of emotional manipulation is to keep it as undetected as possible. This section aims to blow this secret world wide open for all to understand.

Love Bombing

Love bombing is a technique typically used by emotional manipulators at the start of their interaction with a victim. It involves the intense, sudden, and forceful display of positive feelings toward a victim. This may seem counterintuitive at first. If a person is trying to harm someone, why do they act so intensively positive at first? Because it serves their own objectives!

The theory behind love bombing is it creates an intense feeling of trust, affection, and compliance from a victim to their manipulator. The extent to which love bombing is used, and the people it is used on, depends upon the manipulator's assessment of the situation. A victim who is lonely, desperate, and seeking support and comfort is likely to be love bombed more intensely and overtly as the manipulator feels they will be receptive to it. Similarly, a more grounded victim will require a less intense and more subtle onslaught of positivity.

Two important lessons about CEM can be learned from the description of the love bombing technique. First, it illustrates perfectly the covert nature of CEM. Imagine trying to recognize love bombing as something negative. "Well, this person was really nice to me, and made me feel really good." Such a statement is unlikely to trigger any red flags or warning signs of abuse taking place. This is a textbook illustration of how something with a negative outcome can be disguised as something positive.

The second general lesson related to CEM we can learn from understanding love bombing is how CEM is calibrated to the unique situation each target presents. Experienced manipulators will have covertly controlled many people in their past and will have learned from each experience. They therefore know the right intensity, and timing, of any given CEM technique in any given situation.

For example, everyone responds differently to various "loving" gestures. Compliments work well on some, while gifts have more of an effect on others. If someone who was not experienced within the field of CEM attempted to love bomb a target it is unlikely they would have much success in doing so. This is because it requires an understanding of the precise extent to which a victim will respond to certain techniques and not others. Just as a Dr. is able to prescribe the right cure in the right dose, the dark manipulator is able to use the right manipulation in the right amount.

Reinforcement - A CEM Stacked Sequence

Intermittent positive reinforcement is a technique that often follows love bombing chronologically. It is a way of controlling a victim without them realizing what is occurring. The typical sequence of a textbook CEM scenario involves love bombing, followed by positive reinforcement, followed by intermittent positive reinforcement. The reason for this sequence will now be made clear.

Love bombing is the unconditional, unearned, and intense display of positivity from a manipulator to their target in the earliest days of their interaction. It has the purpose of softening up a victim's defenses, increasing their reliance on the person manipulating them and setting the frame of a positive relationship, friendship, or whatever other form the interaction takes.

The next step after love bombing is often positive reinforcement. This is a switch of behavior in which the manipulator no longer displays relentless, unconditional positivity toward their victim. Instead, the manipulator withholds any positivity whatsoever until a time when the victim is performing a desired behavior. So, for example, if the manipulator wants their victim to call them frequently, the manipulator will only show a positive response when this happens. The victim will be unaware that positive attention is being used strategically against them, but will subconsciously comply with the wishes of the manipulator to experience the good feelings on offer.

This predictable positive reinforcement is then replaced by intermittent positive reinforcement, or IPR. IPR involves the withholding of expressions of positivity, even when a desired behavior is displayed. For example, if the manipulator wants their victim to offer to buy them things, and the victim complies, the manipulator will only reward this desired behavior with a positive emotional response some of the time.

This unpredictability causes a deep, subconscious craving for positive attention on behalf of the victim, without the victim ever having conscious knowledge of what is happening. The victim will then begin to chase a good reaction from the manipulator by any means possible. The manipulator has their victim behaving in a certain way and the victim will have no awareness whatsoever of what they are doing or why they are doing it.

The preceding sequential technique of love bombing, positive reinforcement, and finally intermittent positive reinforcement illustrates one way a covert emotional manipulator can deploy positive expression and cold withdrawal to sculpt the emotional response of their victims. Reality denial is a CEM technique that initially impacts upon the mind, rather than the emotions, of the victim. The consequences, however, can devastate a victim's emotions, as you are about to see.

Reality Denial

One of the most terrifying experiences a human can endure is the feeling of losing their own sanity. This is bad enough if it can be explained by something understandable, such as mental illness or the temporary byproduct of stress, but is even more unsettling if the feeling of insanity has been covertly induced by an emotional manipulator.

Reality denial refers to a range of CEM techniques that all have the same purpose— destroying a victim's sanity to serve the manipulator's own selfish aims. The ways reality denial takes place, and its impact, will now be explored in greater detail.

One of the main principles underpinning reality denial is graduality. Manipulators are unlikely to instantly aim for the total destruction of a victim's sanity, as such an outcome is almost impossible to achieve without being detected. Instead, skilled manipulators tend to take the "slowly but surely" approach. This involves the gradual erosion of a person's sanity until their trust in their own faculties is standing upon the flimsiest of foundations.

So how does a covert manipulator begin the process of eroding a victim's sanity? It often starts with the small-scale undermining of a victim's confidence in their own memory. The manipulator will engineer various situations in which a victim is left questioning their own recollection of events. The manipulator will always ensure that their own portrayal of what really happened is the one that ends up seeming the most credible.

This process of minor confidence erosion actually serves two covertly manipulative purposes simultaneously. First, it reduces the victim's trust in their own powers of recall and understanding. Second, this trust is transferred onto the manipulator instead. It is important to note that this will never seem like a big deal at first. The manipulator will simply come across as the person with the slightly better memory. The victim will even be thankful they have someone whose recollection they can rely on!

Over time, the covert emotional manipulator will increase the severity of the events they make the victim question. What starts as seemingly harmless and insignificant will be amplified into a victim losing all confidence in their own cognitive powers. The most insidious element of this process is the victim's tendency to blame their own mind for the loss of ability. Skilled manipulators will also be the ones pulling the strings but never, ever letting the victim become aware of what is really taking place.

Chapter 2: Dark Persuasion

Persuasion - The Dark Side

Persuasion is a topic that is written and talked about a lot. A large number of articles and books exist to help people become more persuasive. Does this mean that every persuasive person is a dark manipulator? Far from it. There is a definite distinction between persuasion and dark persuasion.

Any attempt by someone to influence a person to do something can be seen as persuasion. There are many legitimate uses of persuasion that are anything but dark psychology. If a negotiator persuades a terrorist to let some hostages ago, or a police officer talks a suicidal person down from a ledge, persuasion has taken place. This type of persuasion can be understood as "positive persuasion." So what exactly would qualify persuasion as "dark"?

The DNA of Dark Persuasion

The first difference between dark and positive persuasion is the motive. Positive persuasion is only used to encourage someone to do something that won't harm them. The example of the negotiator shows that positive persuasion can even save lives. The motive for dark persuasion is vastly different.

Dark persuasion lacks any form of moral motive. The motive is instead sometimes amoral and mostly immoral. If positive persuasion can be understood as helping people help themselves, dark persuasion can be viewed as the process of making people act against their own self-interest. Sometimes people will do so begrudgingly, aware that they may not be making the best choice, but eager to stop the incessant persuasion efforts. Other times, the best dark persuaders will be able to make someone think they are acting wisely, when in reality they are doing the exact opposite.

So what are the main motivations for dark persuaders? It depends upon the type of individual doing the persuading. Some people seek to persuade others to serve their own self-interests. Others act through the sole malicious intention of pure harm. They may not benefit by darkly persuading someone, but they do so anyway, purely for the purpose of inflicting pain upon their victim. Others enjoy the sense of control that dark persuasion provides them with.

The outcome of dark persuasion also differs from positive persuasion. Positive persuasion will typically result in one of three scenarios: benefit to the person being persuaded, a win/win benefit to the persuader and the persuaded, or a mutual benefit for the persuaded person and a third party. All of these outcomes involve a positive result for the person being persuaded. Sometimes others benefit, sometimes not. There is no situation in which only the persuader benefits, however.

Dark persuasion has a very different set of outcomes. The persuader always benefits, either directly, or through exercising their distorted need for control and influence. The person being persuaded goes against their own self-interest and does not benefit from being persuaded. Finally, the most skilled dark persuaders are able to not only harm their victim and benefit themselves, but also harm others in the process. Let's take the example of a dark persuader who talks someone into committing suicide so the persuader can profit from an insurance policy. Not only has the persuader gained financially, but the victim has lost their life and also hurt anyone who knew or cared about them.

Unmasking the Dark Persuaders

So who exactly is using these dark methods of persuasion?

The main characteristic of a dark persuader is either an indifference toward or inability to care about how persuasion impacts others. Such people are either totally narcissistic and see their own needs as far more important than others' needs, or sociopathic and unable to even grasp the concept of someone else's emotions.

You'll often find dark persuasion in a relationship. One, or, in the worst-case scenario, both partners are inclined toward darkly persuading the other. If such attempts are persistent and enduring, the relationship can be considered psychologically abusive. Some examples of relationship dark persuasion include stopping the other partner from taking new job opportunities or pursuing personal leisure. The dark persuader will convince the victim that they are acting "for the good of the relationship." In reality, the victim is simply hurting both themselves and the relationship. The relationship is harmed as the dark persuader gains increasing certainty at being able to manipulate their victims.

Dark Persuasion Tactics

So how exactly do dark persuaders carry out their wishes? Some people might question the notion that such a harmful thing as dark persuasion actually occurs. They would be wrong. The reason it can be executed is because of the skill of the persuaders. They are experts in disguising the nature of what is occurring. These are their tactics.

The Long Con

The Long Con is a type of slow, drawn-out method of persuasion. Some of the main reasons people are able to resist persuasion include a feeling that they are being pressured, or a lack of trust or rapport with the person who is seeking to persuade them. The Long Con is able to overcome both these problems.

The Long Con involves the dark persuader taking their time to earn their victim's trust. They will carefully befriend their victim and make sure the victim likes and trust them. This is usually achieved by excessive, artificial rapport building, and other ways of increasing comfort levels.

As soon as the victim has been sufficiently readied psychologically, the persuader begins their attempts. These usually start with some insincere positive persuasion. The persuader will lead their victim into making some choices, or carrying out some actions, that are actually for their own benefit. This has a twofold purpose. First, the victim becomes accustomed to being persuaded by their persuader. Second, the victim makes a mental association between the persuasion and a positive outcome.

So how is The Long Con executed? Let's take an example victim, a recently widowed lady, vulnerable due to age and bereavement.

Following her loss, she is befriended by a man, perhaps a relative, perhaps a member of her church. He shows immense kindness and patience with her, so over time, her guard drops when she's around him.

This man then carries out small acts of positive persuasion, such as advising her of a better bank account, or a way to reduce her monthly bills. The victim appreciates these efforts and trusts his advice. The man then darkly persuades her to let him invest some of her money. Trustingly, she obliges. The man of course takes everything he can from her. If he is skilled, she will end up feeling as though he genuinely tried to help her, and just had bad luck. Such is the depth of dark persuasion.

Graduality

When people hear about acts of dark persuasion, such as individuals being talked into suicide or murder, it seems unbelievable. Who would do such a thing? People fail to realize that dark persuasion isn't always a big, sudden request out of nowhere. Dark persuasion should instead be understood as a staircase. The persuader will make the victim take one step at a time. This doesn't seem like a big deal. Before they know it, they are a long way down, and the persuader isn't going to let them back up.

So how would graduality look in real life? Let's take the example of a psychopathic criminal who wished to make others commit crimes for them. If you can't imagine such a person, think of gang bosses, cult leaders, or Charles Manson.

This psychopathic criminal wouldn't begin by asking a person to murder. Far from it. They might start by carrying out a little petty crime or hiding a weapon for their persuader. No big deal. Over time though, the acts the manipulator persuades their victim to commit become increasingly severe. The persuader also has the unseen leverage of being able to hold the smaller misdeeds over the victim. Before they know it, the victim has a feeling of being in too deep. They can easily be persuaded to carry out even the most shocking crimes, because in their minds, they have no other choice.

Dark persuaders are experts at using graduality to increase the severity of their persuasion over time. They know that their victims would never jump across a canyon. So, instead, the persuaders build them a bridge, bit by bit.

Masking True Intentions

There are several ways persuaders are able to use dark psychological principles to get what they want. Disguising the true desires of the manipulator is an important step in a successful dark persuasion. The best persuaders can use this approach in different ways depending on their victim and circumstance.

One dark psychological principle used by the best persuaders is the knowledge that many people find it difficult to refuse two requests in a row. Let's say a manipulative person wants to extract $200 from their victim, which they have no intention of repaying. The persuader may begin by explaining why they need a loan for $1000 and detailing the serious and severe consequences that will happen if they don't borrow it.

The victim may feel some form of compassion or guilt toward the persuader and wish they could help. However, they explain that $1000 is more than they can afford to lend. The persuader will then lessen their request to the original sum of $200 that they actually wanted. They will have an emotional reason, such as the $200 at least keeping the lights switched on for another few weeks. The victim feels too awkward and unable to refuse this second request. The persuader gets their $200 as originally intended and the victim will not know what has taken place.

Reverse psychology, of a type, is another way to mask true intentions during the course of persuasion. Some people have a personality known as a "boomerang." This means they will refuse to go in the direction they are thrown, and instead, veer off in the opposite direction.

If a dark persuader knows someone is a boomerang type then they have identified a key weakness. Let's take, for example, a persuader whose friend is attempting to win over a certain girl. The persuader knows that the friend will use this girl and hurt her. The girl is torn between the malicious friend and an innocent third party. The persuader will deftly steer the girl in the direction of the guy who will actually be good for her, knowing that she will go against this and choose the harmful friend.

Leading Questions

As anyone who has ever encountered a skilled salesman will know, verbal persuasion can be very impactful when deployed in a careful and calibrated way. One of the most powerful techniques in the verbal arsenal of a dark persuader is the use of leading questions. These are questions intended to trigger a particular response in their victim. For example, a leading persuader may ask their target something like "so how bad do you think those people are?" The question implies that the people he is asking about are definitely bad to one extent or the other. This contrasts with the non-leading question of "how do you feel about those people?"

Dark persuaders use leading questions, such as those described above, in a very careful way. Any dark persuader with a little experience is well aware of the fact that, if the victim begins to get the sense they are being led, they will resist and become less easily persuaded. If the persuader begins to sense the victim is aware of what is happening, they will switch tactics immediately, and only return to the leading questions after the victim has calmed down and they have regained their influential state.

The Law of State Transference

State is a concept that refers to the general mood a person is in. If someone is aligned in their thoughts, words, and deeds, then this is an example of a strong, congruent state. The law of state transference involves the concept of the person who holds the balance of power in any given situation being able to transfer their emotional state onto the person they are interacting with. This is a powerful concept when used by a dark persuader.

If someone is trying to carry out persuasion, and is aware of the law of state transference, there is a particular technique they can use to influence the level of control they hold over their target. The technique is as follows: Initially, the influencer will force their own state to match the natural state of their target. If the target is sad, and talking slowly, the influencer will force their own state into this same format. By doing so, they create a rapport on a deep, subconscious level with their target.

After a "state match" has been carried out, the influencer will begin to subtly alter their own state to assess how much compliance they have from their victim. For example, the persuader may slightly speed up their tone of voice to judge whether their victim will match their own pace. If the victim shows signs of compliance then this is a clear indication that the influencer has reached the "hook point."

Once the hook point has been reached, the influencer will change their own state to the one they wish their victim to have. This could be happy and positive or angry and indignant, depending upon which state will best serve the influencer's aims at the time. This technique shows the impact of subconscious cues on the success or failure of any given persuasion.

Chapter 3: Undetected Mind Control

Not All Mind Control Is Undetected

A mind is a person's sanctuary. No matter what else may be lost to others, a human mind is its owner's and owner's alone. Right? Wrong.

People like to think they are fully in control of their own thoughts and actions. That their mind is as much under their own control as their right hand is. But is this really the case? When you are dreaming, are you in careful control of your dreams? If you can't concentrate, are you choosing your distracting thoughts?

Our minds are actually incredibly susceptible to influence and being controlled. Think about when you are watching a horror movie. Your mind and emotions are being led and influenced by the music, lighting, and choice of camera shot. Even though you know you are watching a movie, your brain still responds to the prompts it is given. If the brain can be influenced so strongly by something we have chosen and are aware of, how strong would the influence be of a skilled, dark, psychological manipulator?

Undetected mind control is the most deadly type of mind control in existence. If someone is aware that their mind is being influenced then they can object mentally, verbally or physically. They can avoid contact with the controlling person or situation. A lot of people would run at the first sign of a dangerous person trying to get inside their brain and take it over. If their mind controller is undetected, like a stealth bomber, then it is not possible for the victim to put their defenses up in time.

There are two types of tactics for taking over a person's mind undetected—interpersonal interactions, and the use of media. Traditionally, media mind control was only possible for large companies, and individual mind controllers were left to interpersonal mind control only. Nowadays, this is no longer the case. Laptops and smartphones have placed media mind control powers directly into the hands of the coldest manipulators walking the Earth.

Before we learn about the specific tactics used in the pursuit of undetected mind control, we must learn about the manipulative people who use such tactics. Like all dark psychological manipulators, undetected mind controllers have the desire to influence others, usually for their own benefit.

Undetected mind controllers are often more cowardly and logical than other manipulators, however. Unlike impulsive psychopaths, undetected mind controllers are likely to only act after careful consideration. To control someone's mind in a way that remains undetected is no easy endeavor. It requires deliberate knowledge and application. Because of this, mind controllers are patient and cunning people. They also fear being caught out so they aim to hide their methods as much as possible. They are like hidden puppet masters, pulling their victims' strings from behind a curtain.

Undetected Mind Control Tactics

Let's learn about the specific methods used by manipulators to control a victim's mind in an undetected way. We will explore both the interpersonal and media techniques that comprise a manipulator's toolkit. Examples will be provided of how such techniques can be used on an individual, or broader collective scale.

Finding Those In Need

One of the first and most important tactical principles of undetected mind control is finding a victim with a goal. It has been proven, both scientifically and anecdotally, that a person who has a pressing need or desire is more susceptible to undetected mind control than someone who feels at ease and satisfied. This can range from a small, physical goal such as feeling thirsty and seeking a drink, to a large, psychological goal, such as craving love and affection.

Think of someone who is looking for another person in a crowd. They will manage to filter out all the people who are not their goal and hone in on the one who is. The brain is similar. If there is something it needs or wants, it is able to direct a person toward it, even if they are unaware any control is taking place. The best mind controllers will discreetly find out what a victim's goals are and seek to manipulate them with these in mind.

One classic example of the susceptibility of people with a goal is an experiment conducted in subliminal influence. Subliminal influence is another name for undetected mind control. Two sets of people were shown a film with a hidden image of an iced tea. One set of people were thirsty, the others not. When given the chance to purchase a specific drink from a selection, the thirsty individuals purchased the iced tea in greater numbers than would be expected statistically. This is evidence that, when a person's brain is desperate for something, it will gladly take suggestions on what to choose.

So how does this principle work on an individual, interpersonal level? If a mind controller finds a victim who is desperately craving something in their life, usually the fulfillment of some deep emotional need, the manipulator will be able to control their mind with greater ease. If, for example, a victim has recently suffered a romantic relationship breakup, it is likely their psyche is craving company. The mind controller will influence their target into thinking that they are the victim's savior when, in reality, they are likely to be their ruin.

Some of the most common areas of need a manipulator will seek to exploit include a person's need for monetary stability, their need to belong, and their need for company. These vulnerabilities can be exploited by an experienced manipulator for a number of purposes. The manipulator may seek to sexually or financially exploit their victim. They may seek to gain their allegiance to some form of cult or ideologically extreme movement. They may simply toy with the victim for their own sadistic pleasure.

Restricting Choice

Restricting choice is a verbal form of undetected mind control. It is a very subtle form of dark psychology, because it provides the manipulator with a range of built-in "get out clauses" should their victim turn suspicious. The key to this particular form of mind control is to take away any real choice that a victim has regarding a particular circumstance while maintaining the illusion that the victim was in control all along.

The restriction of choice is similar to a popular and powerful sales technique known as the choice close. We will use an example to illustrate this process, clearly identifying the difference between someone behaving in a psychologically normal way, and a dark manipulator who seeks only to serve their own purpose at the expense of others.

Take the scenario of a woman being asked out on a date. A regular guy might work up the courage to ask his question, lacking confidence or certainty, and then finally stammer out an open-ended question, such as "Would you like to go out with me?" Such a question leaves a clear possibility for a response of "No." This is the usual way things go for people who are not familiar with the use of dark psychological principles.

Someone who knows how to control someone's mind in an undetected way, however, will approach the same scenario very differently. They like to confidently and smoothly charm their victim, to get them laughing and lowering their guard. Then, with total confidence and assurance, the manipulator will ask "So, am I taking you out on Thursday or Saturday?" The limited choice presented to the victim, who is in a psychologically soft state due to the charm, will almost always result in the victim choosing between Thursday or Saturday. Answering "No" was never an option.

The diabolical aspect of the above technique is that, unlike other forms of mind control, such as those aided by media, there is no tangible evidence of the words a person has spoken. If, somehow, the victim picks up on the restriction of choices by the manipulator, the manipulator can respond in two ways—a denial or a reframe.

A denial allows the manipulator to insist they do not offer a limited choice, and that the victim is remembering things wrongly or worrying too much.

A reframe can allow the manipulator to put the victim on the back foot by saying something like "I can't believe you're analyzing my words so much. That really hurts me, and makes me not want to open up to you." Both the denial and the reframe are effective emergency escape plans for the manipulator who is caught out.

Media Mind Control - Images

Just as our five senses are our guides in life, they can also be our enemies and traitors. Our sense of sight and the visual processing areas of the brain are very powerful. We almost always dream visually, even if another sense is missing, and we usually picture someone we are remembering rather than associating some other sensory input with them. This makes imagery and visual manipulation a particularly powerful technique of media mind control.

Traditionally, media production was in the hands of companies and institutions. These manipulative entities were able to pioneer the use of visual, subliminal mind control. Examples include split-second pictures of a product or person inserted into a seemingly innocent movie. Such split-second images, which the person perceives as nothing more than a flash of light, are able to take powerful control of a person's emotions. They have been used as recently as 21st century Presidential elections.

Worryingly, such devastatingly impactful imagery techniques are now in the hands of individual manipulators. Even worse, such techniques can now be tailored to a specific victim. If the victim has a particular fear of or aversion to something, the manipulator can subtly use the feared image to access and warp a person's emotions without them knowing.

Let's look at an example of individual imagery mind control. We live in the age of Smartphones and video. Everything can shoot high definition clips at the touch of a screen and send them at blistering speeds to someone else. High-tech manipulators are therefore able to allude to feared images. For example, if a manipulative boyfriend is aware that his girlfriend has a deep fear of insects, he may "accidentally" place a book with a picture of an insect on its cover in the background during a video chat. The girlfriend is unlikely to consciously register the book's presence, but on a subtle, emotional level, she will be feeling its impact.

Media Mind Control - Sound

Sound is another way in which a person is vulnerable to undetected mind control. Both experiments and personal experience will confirm this to you. Have you ever had a song stuck in your head? How easy was it to get rid of? The sound had a powerful influence over you, even though you knew it was present. The power of audio manipulation is even greater when it is undetected. Experiments have shown that if restaurant customers are exposed to music from a particular region, they are more likely to order wine from that country. When questioned, they had no idea that something as simple as sound had steered their decision.

One famous example of media mind control using sound is the hiding of words and phrases in songs and other media containing a soundtrack. There have been lawsuits aiming to prove that musicians hide occult references in their work, and to ban them from doing so. This has also happened, with more serious impact, beyond the world of entertainment media.

Governments have sometimes used audio mind control as a form of brainwashing. For example, in North Korea, people are forced to listen to patriotic songs at regular intervals. These embed themselves deep inside a person's mentality and affect an unseen influence. For a less extreme example, think of advertising jingles. If a person is prompted by the sound of a famous jingle, like the McDonald's "I'm lovin it" melody, the person usually repeats the advertising message on autopilot.

Audio undetected mind control can also be used by individual manipulators. There is a range of interpersonal influence tactics using auditory mind control of varying types. Even if you know the tactics, it is still difficult to recognize them being executed. This is because of their stealthy, underhand nature.

One of the creepiest forms of auditory mind control is subliminally influencing a person as they sleep. Have you ever seen those CDs and tapes that are played during sleep to help people to stop smoking? A skilled mind controller is the evil equivalent of such products. When a victim is at their most vulnerable, and totally lets their guard down by sleeping, the manipulator will take this chance to implant their dark and devious commands in a person's ear and let them sink into the deepest layers of the brain.

Another form of interpersonal auditory mind control is masking words with similar sounding words or noises. Have you ever seen the film American Psycho? Although it's fiction, it shows genuine mind control techniques. The main character, serial killer Patrick Bateman, blatantly tells his victims what he does: "I'm in executions and murders." When questioned as to what he said, he calmly responds, "I'm in acquisitions and mergers." The subliminal influence is already in the person's psychological recesses.

Sounds that are outside the range of human perception are a form of auditory mind control that both individuals and organizations can use. Such sounds, which are particular frequencies, impart deep feelings of terror, dread, or unease into those who are exposed to them unknowingly. Although widely used in horror movies, some innovative mind controllers have successfully used such sounds to impact the emotional stability and wellbeing of their victims.

Chapter 4: Mind Games

Mind Games - Always Dark?

"Mind games" is one of the most commonly heard expressions in this book. Unlike many other dark psychological traits that feature in these pages, mind games are something many people would claim to understand and recognize in the course of their everyday life. People are rarely able to accurately recognize and understand mind games, however. Just as many people say the phrase "I feel depressed" without meeting the psychological definition for depression, many people feel they understand mind games when really they have no idea what this means.

Some people will attribute a wide range of normal behavior to "mind games." For example, if someone is teasing them or hinting at some kind of surprise, they will say the person is playing mind games. This is untrue, at least within the world of dark psychology. The intentions of someone playing genuinely dark mind games are not good, positive, or friendly. Therefore, innocent "games" such as teasing and surprises fall outside of the mind games categorization right away.

So if innocent "games" are not mind games in the dark psychology sense of the term, what exactly are? Mind games are any type of psychological scheme on behalf of a manipulator toward the victim that is intended to play games with the victim's sanity and willpower. This differs from other types of dark psychological manipulation in the sense that the manipulator is often "toying" with the victim. The manipulator is less invested in the outcome than they are in some other types of manipulation, and has less regard for the severity of the situation.

A dark mind game can therefore be understood as one played by the manipulator for their own amusement and delight without any regard for the victim's wellbeing. Depending on the type of mind game, the intention is often to "test" the victim and explore their psyche, just as a child would "test" and "try out" a new toy. The best dark psychological mind games are played without their true nature apparent being apparent. This can make them difficult to detect and very destructive to deploy.

The Motivation Behind Mind Games

In exploring the difference between mind games that are dark and those that are not we touched upon the motivation behind manipulative mind games. The range of motivations that underpin manipulative mind games will now be explored more fully. This shows the spectrum of dark motivation that underpins this commonly found manifestation of dark psychology.

One reason for the playing of mind games is to manipulate the victim into performing a behavior or thinking or feeling a certain way. The manipulator, in this situation, may feel that their other forms of manipulation are not effective and may try something less obvious, such as a mind game. The manipulator may also choose to influence their victim in this way for their own twisted amusement. This occurs if the manipulator is trying to get pleasure as well as influence as a result of their mind game deployment.

The specific types of influence that can be attained by playing mind games will be explored in further detail in this chapter's next section. Basically, mind games are good for reducing a victim's certainty and psychological strength in a very subtle way that is hard to perceive. Mind games can also be used to achieve influence while maintaining the victim's illusion of autonomy.

Influencing a victim is far from the only motivation behind the playing of mind games, however. Many manipulators play mind games as a form of entertainment and for no deeper purpose whatsoever. They enjoy and derive pleasure from plotting a way to impact a victim's psychology and watching the victim succumb to their intentions. Such manipulation is similar to a form of sociopathic detachment. Manipulators of this type are able to ignore the fact that their victim is an equal human being with feelings and thoughts. Instead, the manipulator simply sees the victim as a system that exists to be figured out and manipulated for fun. This form of mind game is particularly dangerous, as victims can be driven to suicide simply to amuse the person playing games with them.

Sometimes, dark psychological mind games are played as a formed of learned behavior rather than representing any kind of conscious intent on the part of the manipulator. This happens when the manipulative individual has simply been exposed to such mind games throughout the course of their life and knows no other way.

This may be seen as somehow innocent, but it is not. Just because someone does something evil automatically does not absolve them of the moral responsibility of doing so. In some ways, the manipulators who play dark mind games without having to think about it are the most dangerous. They do not know any other option, so have no prospect of reforming and becoming more balanced human beings as a result.

The Dark Psychologist's Playbook - Main Mind Games Explained

Now that we understand the difference between a dark psychological mind game and a regular mind game it is important to explore the specific types of mind games that are found. Much like the overall concept of mind games, the specific games people play often have innocent and dark variants. Knowing which are examples of dark psychology and which part of everyday life is essential to understanding this particular facet of dark psychology.

Ultimatums

What exactly is an ultimatum? It is when one person presents another with a severe choice. This typically takes the form of a demand worded as "Do this…or this will happen." Some examples include "Quit smoking…or I will leave you" or "Lose weight…or I will see other people." Ultimatums are any type of "request" that is actually closer to a "demand." Ultimatums are one of the main forms of dark psychological game playing, but this does not mean that every ultimatum is a mind game!

The three factors that determine whether an ultimatum can be understood as "dark psychology" are the type of person issuing the ultimatum, their intention for doing so, and the nature of the ultimatum itself. Each of these three aspects will now be explored in turn to provide a comprehensive picture of the ultimatum manipulation tactic and its use.

The person issuing an ultimatum is a key factor as to whether an ultimatum is a manifestation of dark psychology or not. In the example of a legitimate, non-dark ultimatum, the person issuing it will often have a valid and genuine care about the person they are attempting to help. Examples of some possible legitimate individuals include a person's close relative, sibling, or spouse. Just because someone falls into one of these categories, however, does not automatically mean their ultimatum is free of dark psychology!

The motivation behind the ultimatum is another key element of how to understand it. People who issue ultimatums with a good intention are motivated by the desire to help or make something better in someone's life. This could be to improve their health or stop them from carrying out a bad habit. An example of a well-motivated ultimatum may include "Don't drink as much or I can't be around you" or "Let's go to the gym together or it won't be appropriate to have any more kids." Such ultimatums are issued with the intention and purpose of helping someone make a good choice and carry out some type of behavior that has a positive life impact.

Judging the intention of an ultimatum is difficult, however, and for this reason it is not always possible to identify a darkly manipulative ultimatum from the intention behind it. Instead, the nature of the ultimatum itself is often the best way to figure out whether it is manipulative or not. Dark psychological ultimatums will often involve the person being requested to perform them acting against their own self-interest or doing something that violates their personal morals. In aiming for this outcome, the manipulator is able to test the extent to which their victim is willing to go against what they believe in. On the contrary, good ultimatums will not require a person to do anything harmful or anything that goes against their own conscience.

By now, you should be able to understand what a "good" ultimatum looks like, in terms of the person issuing it, their motivation for doing so and the purpose of the ultimatum itself. So what is a textbook example of a darkly psychological ultimatum?

The first hallmark of a dark psychology ultimatum is the person who is issuing it. They will often not have a valid status within their victim's life. For example, the ultimatum giver may be someone the victim is having an illicit romance with, the victim's boss, or a friend who has far too much psychological influence and control over a victim. They can also take a valid role within the victim's life, such as being a spouse, parent etc. If they are someone on the edges of a person's social circle, and are issuing ultimatums, it is an indication that dark psychology is being deployed.

So what kind of ultimatums do such darkly psychological people issue? Some examples include ultimatums that are harmful to the person presented with them or that go against the person's moral character. Let's picture a victim who has an aversion to drinking alcohol for either health or ethical reasons. The manipulator will note this aversion and recognize it as a source of amusement and pleasure for their own dark mind. The manipulator will then use the idea of alcohol as a basis for ultimatums with which to bend and twist their victim's will. Some examples of these ultimatums include "Do a shot with me or I'm going home" or "Either drink or don't bother coming to the party. You won't be welcome there."

Some of the most extreme ultimatums can involve self-harm, suicide, or even murder. For example, the manipulator may tell the victim "cut your arm, or I will cut mine three times." A manipulative girlfriend may issue an ultimatum to her boyfriend telling him to "Kill this other man or I will leave you, because it will prove you don't care for me." At the most extreme end of the spectrum, people are manipulated into taking their own life under the pretense of a suicide pact. Once the victim has died, the manipulator does not carry out their side of the bargain.

The Eternal Breakup

One of the fundamental requirements for a happy, peaceful, and stable romantic relationship is a feeling of security and contentment. People in happy romances or marriages feel at ease and do not feel a sense of constant threat that their relationship might come to an end at any time. Masters of dark psychology are aware of these principles and do everything possible to invert them for their own twisted aims. By cultivating a sense of instability, chaos, and negativity within a relationship, the manipulator is able to ensure that their victim is as powerless as possible.

"The Eternal Breakup" is one of the most common and effective manipulation mind games used within a romantic context to cause instability and anxiety. What exactly is it? It is the persistent and prolonged use of threatening to leave someone. This may take the form of implied break ups, promised break ups, or actual break ups that are not followed through on. Examples for each of these types of tactic, as well as the impact they have, will now be carefully considered.

Implied breakups are those that do not actually involve the overt mention of breaking up. Instead, the manipulator hints at the breakup to plant the seed of doubt in their victim's mind. The manipulator may casually mention future plans that do not involve the person they are with. They may hint at an active breakup, such as by stating "Well, I won't put up with that for long" or some other kind of veiled hint. Any type of action or sentence that has the impact of making the victim doubt the relationship's longevity counts as an implied breakup.

The "promised breakup" is a step between an implied breakup and an actual breakup. This is where the manipulator issues threats toward their victim and overtly states they intend to break up with the victim in the future. For example, in the course of a discussion, the manipulator may say something like "I am going to leave you soon and I won't have to deal with this anymore." Any instance where the manipulator mentions the idea of a breakup, separation, or divorce without actually carrying out the step itself is an example of a promised breakup.

The "actual breakup," which fails to occur, is the final example, and most severe, of the "eternal breakup" mind game. This is where the manipulator actually "breaks up" with their victim without following through on it. They may pack a bag to leave, recognize their victim's discomfort and sadness, and then fail to follow through. They may break up with their victim with no intention of ever following through on it only to "accept the victim back" following begging and sadness.

So now that you understand what the "eternal breakup" is and the different forms it can take, let's explore the purpose behind this particular tactic of psychological manipulation and mind games. This mind game is intended to remove feelings of certainty and security from a victim's life, to reduce their power in relation to their manipulator, and instead place the power in the manipulator's own hands. This form of mind game can also be used as an evil "test" by the manipulator. By repeatedly breaking up with their victim, the manipulator is able to gauge the extent to which the victim will put up with being played with. The manipulator is also able to portray themselves as the "compassionate" party by "kindly" agreeing to not break up with a victim if the victim is emotional and begging for a relationship not to end.

So why does this eternal breakup tactic work? Many people, when hearing about the tactic for the first time, think that it does not make sense as any victim would be pleased to break up with a manipulative person! This is a fundamental misunderstanding of dark psychology, however. The victim is not in a psychologically healthy or normal situation so they are not in a position to rationally understand why the relationship should end. Instead, they are vulnerable and susceptible to their manipulator's power and influence. For this reason, they are eager to preserve a relationship that has become nothing more than a dark psychological playground for the manipulator to enjoy.

The repercussions for someone who has been subject to the "eternal breakup" for a long time can be very severe. They are likely to develop incredibly serious trust issues and be unable to trust any other person in any other situation. This can destroy a person's professional and family lives, which, ironically, is exactly what the manipulator desires. After an extremely prolonged period of being "broken up with," the victim is likely to become almost a subservient slave of the manipulator, doing anything they please to avoid the threat of another breakup. Often, at this point, the manipulator loses interest, having completely broken their victim's will. They move on to a new target, leaving only a ruined life in their wake.

Hard To Get

Much like ultimatums, the "hard to get" mind game is one that can easily be confused for normal, healthy behavior. Some fundamental differences exist, however, that show the "hard to get" mind game to be a clear product of dark psychology. The first step to understanding "hard to get" is therefore to understand when it is evil and when it is innocent.

Normal, non-dark psychological use of "hard to get" is as follows: A person will want to seem like a bit of a challenge to someone they are romantically interested in. They will therefore not be too available. This may involve not accepting every suggested date, not replying to messages or phone calls too quickly and other types of similar behavior. This has the intention of keeping the other person interested and eventually leading to a happy romantic relationship together.

A dark psychological deployment of "hard to get" is a lot more dangerous, however. The time when this particular mind game is used tends to differ from its innocent usage and the motivation behind it is also a million miles apart. Users of dark psychological tactics will play "hard to get" at times of the relationship other than the beginning. Their intention will not be to lead to a positive situation and their regard will be for anything other than the victim's wellbeing.

The reason "hard to get" can be used in an innocent way is because it is not violating any expectations at the start of a relationship. People are not dependent or reliant upon the other party and therefore do no harm by being "hard to get." When someone is evasive and unreliable later in a relationship, however, the effects of "hard to get" behavior become a lot more severe. We will now explore the ways in which this can occur and the impact it can have.

Some ways in which a person might play "hard to get" outside a relationship include being unreliable and unavailable after the two partners have already agreed to be in a committed relationship. This is an inversion of the normal dynamic. Normal relationships are often elusive at the start and firmer over time. A manipulator will be artificially firm at the start of a relationship to force a sense of connection, and then will become less and less available over time, once their victim is already "hooked."

When a person plays "hard to get" at a relationship's later stages it makes the other person chase and exert effort to reconnect with the person who is pulling away. This gratifies the manipulator's ego and places power into their hands. The most expert manipulators will balance out their "hard to get" actions with those that convey closeness and reliability. This leads to a deep psychological confusion and instability in the victim's mind, which the manipulator can then exploit for their own purposes.

Chapter 5: Deception

Dark or Not?

Deception is a key aspect of dark psychology. Like many other dark psychological tactics, it can be difficult to tell whether any given instance of deception is dark or not. Before we explore the difference between dark and normal deception, let's first understand exactly what deception is.

A lot of people would state the viewpoint that lying and deception are the same thing. This is inaccurate. Lying is a form of deception but is by no means the only form deception can take. Rather than thinking of deception as "lies" it is better to think of it as "misleading." Any action or word capable of making someone believe something other than the truth can be accurately termed deception.

So what are some common manifestations of deception? Lying, omitting the truth, implying falsehood or fraudulently providing evidence for something false are all examples of deception. You will probably realize that you have done some of these things at some point yourself. Does that mean that all acts of deception are examples of dark psychology? Not at all.

Everyone deceives to some extent or another. People might deceive others for a range of reasons such as kindness, embarrassment or feelings of inadequacy. For example, studies have shown that many, even most men will lie about their height on dating websites. This does not make them practitioners of dark psychology! People even deceive themselves about a range of issues including their health, ambition, and happiness. Such regular, day-to-day examples of deception do not equate to dark deception. So what does?

Deception can be seen as dark when it is carried out with either a negative or indifferent intention toward the person being deceived. Normal deception is usually motivated by an inability to face up to the truth in one way or another. Dark deception, on the other hand, is an understanding that the truth does not serve the deceptive aims of the deceiver. Therefore, the truth is either changed, hidden, or ignored in favor of a version of events that better suits the purpose of the person deceiving.

Put simply, people who deploy dark psychology use deception to harm, not help. They help their own interests, but at any cost, regardless of who gets hurt.

Some people assume that if a deception is small scale it cannot be seen as dark, whereas larger deceptions must be inherently dark. This is not the case. By exploring the idea of the deception spectrum you will see that it is not the size of a deception that determines whether it is dark or not, rather the purpose behind the deception.

The Deception Spectrum

To understand the idea of deception it is important to understand that it can occur on either a large or a small scale. One of the main mistakes that people often make is assuming that deception is only serious if it is big and does not matter if it is small. This is a grave error. Small deceptions can be used in a powerfully dark way by skilled manipulators and are often more effective than large deceptions. Similarly, some of the largest deceptions ever carried out have been performed by deliberate manipulators to serve their own aims and objectives. Dark examples of various types of deception, large and small, will now be presented to illustrate the idea of the deception spectrum.

So what are some of the ways that smaller deceptions can be used by people who practice the art of dark psychology? Often, small deceptions are used initially to test the victim's gullibility and condition them into believing the deceptive statements and actions of the manipulator. If people are conditioned to believe a range of smaller lies over time, they are more likely to believe a larger lie in the future. This gradual conditioning is not the only way smaller deceptions can be used as a dark psychological weapon.

Smaller deceptions can also be carried out to undermine a victim's trust in their own powers of logic and reason. If a manipulator deceives a victim over small issues, and the victim begins to question what is happening, the victim may well conclude that their suspicion is irrational and they therefore cannot trust their own judgment. Most people are more likely to conclude that their own judgment is faulty, rather than another person is deceiving them over seemingly small issues. Users of dark psychology are aware of this general "trust" that people have and seek to exploit it without mercy.

Large-scale deception can also be an example of dark psychology in practice. One of the largest deceptions possible is to convince someone that you are a different person than you say you are. Not in terms of personality or some other detail. An entire identity. Name, date of birth, everything! The most skilled users of dark psychology are able to persuade other people to buy in entirely into their portrayal of a false identity and background.

Now that it has been shown how manipulative users of dark psychology are able to use the deception spectrum for their own aims, we will explore some of the most common topics and subjects that people are deceived about. We will then look at exactly how these large- and small-scale deceptions are carried out by exploring the specific tactics that are used.

Deceptive Topics

Everyone has heard the old saying that "money is the root of all evil." This is an exaggeration, but money is certainly the route of many deceptions.

Deception and money can cross paths in many different ways. Some people deceive to attain money, others deceive to hide their own money, or lack thereof. Because money is such a common topic, some of its deceptive uses will now be explored.

One of the most common dark psychology deceptions involving money is carried out by the professional beggar. These are individuals that aim to extract money from the public despite having plenty of it. These beggars draw on a number of dark psychological principles to get money from innocent victims. Such beggars have been known to inflict injuries upon their own body to appear more desperate to victims. Some of the most extreme deceivers in this area have even turned their own children into heroin addicts to use them as part of their scam. This is an example of the depths that money-related deception can sink to.

Marital status is another common area where people choose to deceive. Sometimes, people try and hide their married background to seduce a new victim. This can be for either financial or sexual or other reasons. Some people have multiple wives spread out across the world who do not know about each other. This type of deception has become harder with the advent of the Internet and the ability to check up on people via social media. The best deceivers are able to hide their tracks expertly and keep each fraudulent wife separate from the next.

Some people choose to appear falsely married when they are in fact not! This type of deception can occur for several reasons. A married couple is often perceived as more trustworthy than a couple that is not married. Some users of dark psychology are aware of this perception and use it for their own schemes and plans. Some people pretend to be married for reasons related to tax and insurance. One of the most common deceptions of this type is the creation of a fictional dead husband or wife to gain people's sympathy and, often, their money as a result.

A criminal background is another area of life many people are deceptive about. This is because it is almost impossible to be trusted professionally or personally if you have committed certain crimes. For example, if a man meets a woman, and the man has committed a serious crime in his past, how likely is he to tell the woman he has just met about this? It seems doubtful that he would be entirely upfront. Interestingly, such deception is not always dark. If the man does it through fear of being rejected, this is not dark deception. If he does it with the intention of hiding the truth to later harm his new victim, then this is a clear indication of dark psychology at work.

One of the most evil and deplorable examples of deception related to criminality is when someone who has committed serious past offences, such as rape, hides these in order to commit similar actions in the future. People with a dark psyche of this type are often compelled by their abnormal urges to the point they will do literally anything to hide the truth and carry on giving in to their compulsions.

Manipulators also feel that deception is a great way to hide any abnormal or socially unacceptable feelings they have. This stops their victim from being alerted to the kind of person they really are until it is too late. For example, if someone who uses dark psychology is interested in a person only for sex, they know this focus is likely to be a red flag to their victim and will therefore deceive their victim. They may either overtly lie or imply that their true intention is love and commitment. The victim falls for the deception, the manipulator's exploitation is complete and yet another person is hurt by deception.

One of the most common areas to be deceptive in is the truth of a manipulator's personal feelings for a victim. Deception is the most powerful tool the manipulator has to influence a victim to perceive things in the way the manipulator wishes, rather than how they really are. Typically, deception will be used in relation to interpersonal feelings to portray the manipulator as something they are not. Some of the most common examples of this use of deception will now be provided.

Within the field of romantic relationships, deception is often used to mask the manipulator's true intentions. Deceptive words and actions will leave a victim feeling as if the manipulator "just happens to be" what they are looking for at that particular time in their life. In actual fact, skilled manipulators are able to identify vulnerable people and probe their psychological needs and weak points. This information can then be used to deceptively cloak the manipulator and make them appear to be something they are not, but something the victim wishes they were. This deception is often the starting point of more complex, long-term manipulations.

Deception can also be used to soften up the victims' feelings in a non-romantic context and increase their susceptibility to manipulation. If, for example, a manipulator is looking for a vulnerable person to use dark psychology against, they may initially portray their own intentions as innocent. Even if the intention is to become intensely close to a person, the manipulator will usually deceptively portray himself as a very casual, easy-going person. This deception can be prolonged if needed. The manipulator will be whatever the victim needs, for as long as the victim needs, in order to get their guard down and allow the thorough manipulation to begin.

Deceptive Tactics

You now understand what exactly dark deception is, its spectrum and the common areas people are deceived about. Now it is time to examine closely the specific tactics used by manipulators to darkly deceive. Each of the tactics is equally powerful and careful manipulators know exactly how to use each at its most impactful and harmful time. It is important to note that manipulators will not neatly alternate between the four following categories—any given deception is likely to involve a blend of each.

Lying is perhaps the most obvious and common form of dark deception. It is likely to be chosen as a technique when the manipulator has decided that their victim is susceptible to lies and unable to gauge the truth. This may be because the victim is a generally trusting person or that the manipulator has carefully worked on their target over time to lower their guard. If a manipulator has chosen to deceive through the use of lies then it is likely they have also thought of a way to hide their lies and explain any discrepancies the victim may notice.

Manipulators are masters of having a "plan b" at any given time during their dark deception.

Deception through lying is likely to occur in a subtle and thought out way. A skilled deceiver is likely to embed their lie into truthful information over time. For example, a manipulator will probably tell a story that is 90% true and 10% false. The victim will perceive the story as entirely true and not have any way of separating and ascertaining the truth regarding the deceptive 10%. Some manipulators also spend time associating truth with a particular tone of voice or gesture. They can then say something falsely deceptive in this tone of voice, or with this gesture, and it is likely to be perceived as true by their victim's subconscious.

Implying is a more subtle form of deception than out and out lying. Implying involves suggesting something false is true rather than boldly stating it is. Let's illustrate this idea with an example. If someone wanted to deceive a victim about the amount of money they have then they could either lie or imply. A lie would sound something like "Oh I'm a successful guy. I've made a lot of money," while the manipulator is well aware this is not the case. An implication may take the form of "it's so stressful trying to handle things with my accountant. Trying to get my tax bill down takes a lot of my time." The manipulator has acted and spoken in a way that implies they are wealthy without flatly stating it.

Manipulators often favor implications, such as those just mentioned, as they provide plausible deniability. If the victim accuses the manipulator of lying, the manipulator can say they did no such thing, and technically be truthful. Implications are also powerful if a victim happens to have an active imagination. The deceptive implication can be seen as a seed planted in the mind of the victim. The victim's own imagination then does the manipulator's work for them and fills in the blank spaces to create an idealized version of reality, according to the manipulator's prompts.

Omission is a failure to mention something that is true. This stands in contrast with other forms of deception such as lies or implications. Both lies and implications use falsehood to cover truth, to varying degrees. Omission instead goes the route of simply ignoring the truth and leading the victim's attention away from it. For example, if a manipulative user of dark psychology had an aspect of their past they did not want their victim to focus on, they would simply never mention it. They would draw attention to other times in their past or swerve the subject whenever possible.

One way omission is often carried out is by creating an "emotional fence" around a situation. This is a tactic in which a manipulator implies that a particular period of their life, or topic, is too painful or uncomfortable to discuss. The victim will then avoid talking about this time, or asking awkward questions, of their own volition. If the victim does bring up the subject the manipulator wishes to avoid then the manipulator can play the "it's too painful" card. This allows them to avoid the truth while making the victim feel guilty for touching on a "painful topic"!

Fraud is the most elaborate and criminal form of deception used by those who deploy dark psychology. Think of fraud as a lie on steroids. Instead of simply lying about something from their past, a fraudulent dark deceiver will have false documents, stories, and other evidence to back up their lie. The most skillful deceivers will use such things in a subtle way. Rather than saying, "no, I really am a Doctor, look at my certificate!" they are likely to make subtle displays such as leaving the fraudulent evidence around for their victims to see for themselves. Deceivers know that if they are too "pushy" with their fraudulent claims then the victim will intuit that something is wrong.

Worryingly, fraud is more common than ever thanks to the prevalence of computers and the Internet. Deceivers are able to use professional-grade software to quickly and easily make realistic-looking documents of almost any type. Such frauds can be carried out for either personal or professional reasons. Some of the most serious types of professional fraud include instances where people have obtained jobs using a false identity, stolen from a company, and then disappeared before their identity can ever be known. Personal frauds include terrifying tales such as people with HIV spreading the disease with the help of falsely produced certificates of clean sexual health.

When dark deception enters the realm of fraudulence it is a sign that the deceiver is a dangerous and committed user of dark psychology. For a person to risk running afoul of the law and facing serious criminal charges, they have to be truly committed to the manipulation they are attempting. If many users of dark deception are amateurs, the deceptive fraudsters are the dangerous professionals that must be avoided at all costs.

Ironically, one of the main ways dark deception is often carried out effectively is following the manipulator's own pantomime of feeling deceived by their victim! Many manipulators know that, by portraying their victim as the deceptive party, they are able to deflect any attention away from their own deceptive efforts. This is an example of a deception within a deception and shows the complex, layered approach to manipulation that many deceivers use.

Chapter 6: Hypnotism

Hypnotism Is Real

Of all the aspects of dark psychology presented in this book, hypnotism is the one most likely to raise eyebrows. When most people hear the word "hypnotism" they think of a guy with a moustache and a top hat waving a pocket watch while insisting someone is "getting very sleepy." Believing in this stereotype is actually dangerous. This is because real hypnotists are out there and are equipped with subtle but powerful techniques. These people are able to draw upon the darkest elements of psychology to influence people in an incredibly powerful way.

So if hypnotism isn't the old stereotypical image of a stage hypnotist, what exactly is hypnosis? Simply put, it is the ability to make suggestions to someone that filter through deep layers of their consciousness. This ability to make deep, impactful suggestions to someone while they are in a vulnerable and suggestible state grants hypnotic dark manipulators a high level of power over their victims. Unlike almost every other technique in this book, hypnotism is not something that people encounter in a milder, more innocent form in their day-to-day lives.

Hypnotism can take the form of both verbal and nonverbal suggestive practices. Often, the forms of suggestion are very subtle and therefore difficult to detect. By its very nature, hypnosis works on the deepest levels of a person's mind. Someone who is skilled in generating a hypnotic state and response in someone will be able to bypass their defenses and influence them without raising any alarms or giving a person a chance to raise their guard.

Hypnotic Tactics

Now that you understand the difference between the stereotype of what hypnosis is, and what it actually is, it is time to explore the main hypnotic tactics. There are many variations on these types of tactics but they offer an insight into the main things to be wary of. Examples of how each tactic can be used will be provided wherever possible to give a clear insight into how hypnotists operate in our midst, undetected, every day.

Suggestion Can Be Silent

If hypnotism, in a darkly psychological sense of the word, can be understood as "deep suggestion," then it is important to understand what exactly is meant by suggestion in this instance. Most people might imagine a suggestion is a clearly stated statement like "I suggest you do this." This is far from the truth. The dark psychology view of suggestion is very far apart from the usual understanding of the word. The first important concept to grasp is the fact that hypnotic suggestion can be either verbal or nonverbal.

Picture the human brain as an iceberg. The part of the iceberg that is above the surface of the water represents the known and understood aspects of cognitive function such as thought. The larger, deeper part of the ice submerged below the water represents parts of the brain that are consciously inaccessible and little understood. If you doubt the power of this hidden portion of the brain you need only think of dreaming and the immense power of the mind to generate series of images, pictures, and sounds while a person is asleep. Dark hypnotists target their efforts toward this hidden, subconscious part of the mind.

There are, broadly speaking, two types of suggestion used by hypnotists—silent and verbal. Both types of hypnotic technique come in a variety of different forms. The exact type of hypnotism a manipulative person chooses to use at any given time depends on a range of factors. Some manipulators will carry out whichever form of hypnotism they feel will be most impactful on their victim's particular psyche. Others carry out whichever technique they happen to wish to use for their own amusement at the time. This depends largely on whether the hypnotist is seeking to exert influence in the most powerful way possible or is merely trying to control someone for their own fun and games.

Verbal suggestion is very difficult to detect. Sometimes, dark hypnotists are able to implant suggestions into their victim's mind using words that sound similar to other, more innocent words.

To take a deeply dark example, if a hypnotist was trying to instill suicidal feelings in their target, they may mask the true command of "You want to die" as something similar sounding such as "You want to dine." The hypnotist would speak the words "you want to die" clearly, but in a context that would mask the true content. For example, the hypnotist could talk about an upcoming trip and state "You have to check out the local restaurants, you want to die, somewhere that is popular but picturesque." The victim's mind would absorb the suggestion of death without consciously understanding why!

The above example of masked verbal suggestions is akin to a poison being hidden in someone's food. The victim consumes the hidden content, thinking that they are enjoying something helpful and innocuous when in actual fact they are absorbing something deadly. The especially devastating part of this technique is the fact the victim will never notice it. Even if someone thought they had picked up on the true words the hypnotist had spoken, imagine how crazy they would sound calling them out! People will generally take whichever option is psychologically easier for them and will therefore accept the masked command without question.

A hypnotist's tone of voice and choice of words is another method of verbal suggestion. Some hypnotists will carefully learn the pace and style of delivery a particular victim uses when they are expressing something serious.

For example, if, when someone wishes to say something meaningful, their voice lowers in pitch and slows in pace, the hypnotist would memorize this detail and retain it for future use. The hypnotist would then make suggestions to the victim in that exact, mirrored tone of voice. Because of the carefully modulated tone, the words delivered in that vocal variation would deeply penetrate a victim's defenses. Because the hypnotist would only deliver the suggestive content in that tone of voice, and then switch back to their usual way of speaking, the victim would be unaware even of what had taken place.

Another form of personalized, verbal suggestion employed by a hypnotic user of dark psychology is to pick up on words that have a special, intense significance for the victim who uses them. For example, when someone is very emotional they will often use a particular term to convey this feeling. If the hypnotic manipulator is able to pick up on these personal words then they are able to deploy them for their own benefit. Just as people have a specific tone of voice, they have a list of personal words of meaning, without often knowing it. The manipulator will understand their victim better than the victim understands herself. Knowing these words and tones, the manipulator can reverse engineer the victim's own brain to use against them.

Suggestion can also take nonverbal forms as well. This can be through the hypnotic manipulator's body language or even cues they place in their environment. If you think such seemingly trivial things could not exert a hypnotic influence then think again! Even political leaders have made use of such tactics in ways such as changing their hairstyle to convey a different intention during speeches. As discomforting as it is to believe, the human mind is deeply susceptible to even the smallest hints and cues.

So what are some of the main ways a hypnotic manipulator can use nonverbal suggestion against their victim? The technique centers around the idea of association. A skilled hypnotist is able to consistently link a strong emotion to some kind of external stimulus such as a particular eye movement they use. For example, if a hypnotist wanted to be able to trigger a feeling of panic in a victim, they may choose to make a particular motion with their eyes whenever the victim was thinking about, or experiencing, panic. The victim's subconscious would then learn to link the eye movement to the feeling. Over time, the hypnotist would be able to trigger the emotional response simply by making the eye movement, even without the need for any other stimulus.

Environmental stimulus is another form of nonverbal suggestion that forms a part of the hypnotist's toolkit. Think of environmental stimulus as like being summoned to the principal's office as a child. The location itself was enough to send you into a feeling of deep panic because you had learned to associate the location with panic and problems. Hypnotists are able to use this same concept to devastating effect in adult life.

For example, they will often be sure to have a certain type of conversation with a victim in one location only. Picture a hypnotist and their victim in a romantic relationship. Every time the hypnotist wishes to get some kind of agreement or consent from his victim, he may be sure to ask her only when they are at a certain coffee shop. Over a period of time, the victim's mind begins to associate the physical environment of the coffee shop with the granting of permission. The hypnotist can then use this physical environment as external psychological leverage whenever he needs to exert influence and control.

Vulnerable Victims

Hypnotism is not equally effective on everybody it is tried on. Some people are more likely to be influenced by a hypnotist than others. Although the exact level of susceptibility is complex and hard to simplify in a single sentence, it boils down to the idea of vulnerability. Vulnerable people are more likely to be agreeable to hypnotic suggestion than people who are less vulnerable. The types of vulnerability sought out by hypnotists in their victims will now be explored along with a guide to how hypnotists exacerbate and magnify the vulnerable paradigm.

The people most vulnerable to hypnotism are those who have recently experienced a significant life-changing event that has reduced their stability and certainty. For example, if a person has just come out of a serious romantic relationship, has suffered bereavement or lost their job, they are particularly vulnerable to suggestion. This is because the human brain craves certainty and understanding above all else. If a hypnotist spots someone who is in a vulnerable place they can offer them certainty and change their vulnerability in general to vulnerability around the hypnotist specifically.

There are roughly two facets of vulnerability in a hypnotist's victim—preexisting vulnerability and exacerbated vulnerability. The most diabolical hypnotists are able to combine both aspects to lethal effect. Not only will the best hypnotic manipulators be able to find someone who is suitably vulnerable, they will find someone who is specifically vulnerable to the hypnotic psychological scheme they have planned.

For example, if a hypnotist is looking to use their powers to gain financially, they might seek out a victim such as a rich, recently bereaved widow. They will then, subtly and over time, associate their own self with feelings of security and comfort while increasing the widow's general feelings of loss and vulnerability. Eventually, the hypnotist is the victim's only refuge from a hell of their own making.

As well as seeking out vulnerability in general, hypnotists are known to seek out situational vulnerability as well. This is when someone is in a situational circumstance that makes them more suggestible than their overall "baseline" of suggestibility. There are tactical tricks a hypnotist can use to ascertain this situational vulnerability. One such tactic is trying to induce "mirroring" behavior in their target. When people feel a subconscious level of connection and rapport with someone they will start to "mirror" the person without knowing they are doing it. To check this, a hypnotist might make some small change to their body language, such as a hand motion. If the victim subconsciously mimics this gesture, then it is a sign the victim is situationally vulnerable.

Now that both general and situational vulnerability have been explored, it is important to understand how the most skilled hypnotists use the two types of vulnerability together for an especially strong impact. If someone is vulnerable in general, due to their life situation, and vulnerable in particular, due to the situation the hypnotist has managed to set up, then that person is in the most influenceable state imaginable. Once such a state has been induced the hypnotist is likely to move on to the most powerful and advanced techniques they possess, such as NLP.

NLP

NLP, or neurolinguistic programming, is a technique that is powerful even in the hands of the most well-intentioned people. Leaders within the world of business and philanthropy are some of the most common advocates of the techniques and principles offered by NLP. Placing such techniques in the hands of people willing to use dark psychology to exploit others is like giving a nuclear weapon to a psychopath. They possess both the power and the will to create serious psychological havoc among their victims. Understanding the main techniques used by practitioners of dark psychology offers insight into the way they can be deployed to devastating impact.

Anchoring

Anchoring is an NLP technique that involves linking an emotional state to some form of external stimulus. If you are familiar with the idea of Pavlovian conditioning, then you will understand this tactic. Hypnotists are able to induce a powerful emotion in a victim and then link it to a stimulus such as a physical gesture or tone of voice. The hypnotist is then able to induce this emotional state at will by performing the linked stimulus.

The most nefarious hypnotists will use the principle of anchoring in a very subtle and underhand way. They will work for a prolonged period of time to induce a variety of different anchors in the psyche of their victim without the victim's conscious awareness of what is taking place. This provides the manipulator with a set of hypnotic puppet strings that they can pull as and when they desire. Often, hypnotists will use an "anchor stack" to induce different intense feelings in quick succession. For example, they will induce the feeling of love, followed by terror, followed by love once more, all in quick succession. This series of emotions overloads the victim's emotional circuitry and leaves them as mere clay in the hands of their controller.

Reframing

Reframing is the art of controlling the way ambiguous information is perceived. There is an old saying that "nothing is good or bad unless we believe it to be." Reframing is the ultimate technique related to this idea. Hypnotists can use reframing to effectively control the way their victim thinks and feels. Think of a skilled reframer as an editor. They are able to selectively choose the victim's focus and the feelings the focus triggers. This is effectively hypnotic mind control.

So how does darkly psychological reframing work in practice? Let's take a situation where a hypnotic manipulator has influenced a victim to no longer spend time around, or communicating with, a particular person. The victim may state feelings of sadness or loss related to this interpersonal change. The hypnotist would be able to reframe these feelings into ones which suited the hypnotist's own purposes. This is best illustrated through an example dialogue.

Victim - "It sucks I haven't spoken to Rachel as much, I miss her."

Hypnotist - "I know you might hate how things are with Rachel, but I know you're smart enough to love the freedom you have now."

Notice how the concept of hate is linked to Rachel and love is linked to the "freedom" of being without her? The hypnotist also plays on the victim's ego by linking the idea of their intelligence to going along with the way the hypnotist wants them to perceive the "frame," or perception, of the facts. Think about what you have already learned about the vulnerability of victims and you will understand how this reframing can be used to devastating impact.

Future Pacing

Future pacing is the closest thing possible to psychologically manipulative time travel. Future pacing allows a skilled manipulator to lead their victim on a mental journey into the future and influence behaviors and responses that will occur in the actual, chronological future that exists independent of the victim's reality.

At its most fundamental, future pacing involves the mental leading of a victim through a future scenario. For example, if the hypnotist wants their victim to feel generous and relaxed whenever they receive money, the hypnotist would ask their victim to envision a situation, such as receiving their next paycheck. To make this future imagining possible the hypnotist would ensure the victim imagined all of their five senses in action—what they would see, feel, touch etc. at the time. This helps the brain to perceive the future scenario as "real" due to its sensory depth.

Once the hypnotist cognitively transports their victim into the future, they begin to suggest certain happenings and monitor the responses. For example, the hypnotist may say something like "Imagine being very generous with this paycheck and providing it to those who really need it, because you are a kind person and doing the right thing is deep in your nature." If the victim's physical response to this future scenario showed signs of compliance and acceptance then the hypnotic manipulator would have the confidence that their victim would actually behave in this way when the scenario occurs in the future.

Due to the intensity and power of the hypnotic techniques mentioned in this chapter, the best manipulators only use them in moderation. For example, a darkly psychological hypnotist would be sure to keep their interaction with a victim 95% normal. This will increase the victim's comfort and trust to such high levels that the 5% time spent on hypnotic influence would not only slip past a victim's defenses unnoticed but would work to great effect once embedded in the victim's mind.

Chapter 7: Brainwashing

Are You Brainwashed About Brainwashing?

If you ask someone if they know what brainwashing is, they will probably reply that they do. Brainwashing is a concept that many people have heard of, while mistaking their vague familiarity for accurate understanding. Before looking at how, where, and why brainwashing occurs, it is essential to understand exactly what brainwashing is and isn't. Of all the dark psychology techniques contained in this book, brainwashing has the most serious and widest impact. If the other dark psychology techniques are sniper bullets, aimed at one particular person, brainwashing is a nuclear bomb capable of devastating an entire city.

The term brainwashing refers to the slow process of replacing a person's ideas about identity and belief with new ideas that are intended to suit the purpose of the person doing the brainwashing. Brainwashing can occur in both wider and narrower contexts. For example, a brainwasher is able to control one person in particular, or use the same techniques and principles to control the minds of a wider group at once. Brainwashing is the process that turns atheists into suicide bombers and prisoners of war into communists. It has been tried, tested, and proven over the years to be effective in almost any scenario.

So what are the most common misunderstandings related to brainwashing? Many people picture the process as some kind of quick and forced occurrence. Picture either Alex in "A Clockwork Orange" or Neo in "The Matrix" having concepts forced into their cranium, involuntarily, in a short space of time. This is Hollywood brainwashing and is far from what actually occurs in real life.

The process of real-world brainwashing will be explored in detail later in this chapter, but at its simplest, brainwashing is a process involving the slow, gradual, and seemingly voluntary changing of a person's "map of reality" from the one they have freely put together to one that is forced upon them by the brainwasher. The evil irony of the technique is the brainwasher will ensure the victim feels in control at all times.

Brainwashing Contexts

So what are some of the main situations that are fertile breeding grounds for brainwashers? Before the process of brainwashing itself is explored fully, let's take a look at the situations in which people are often brainwashed and the motivations behind this.

A lot of people would agree with the idea that "cults brainwash people" but few would be able to explain exactly what a cult is and how they brainwash their recruits. Let's demystify the process. A cult is a fringe group, often built around a charismatic leader who is able to exert high levels of influence over their followers. The cult will usually provide a "complete understanding of reality" to those who follow it. Why exactly is this cult context one in which brainwashing flourishes?

The primary attraction of cults is they present reality as something very simple and within reach of the average person, provided the person is willing to take on board the cult's teachings. We live in a complex modern world where life can seem confusing and overwhelming. Cults cut through this confusion and tell people "don't worry, we have the answer." The way in which this "answer" is presented is intended to play on the human need for belonging and acceptance. Brainwashing can flourish in this context as a result of the idea of the "new normal."

What exactly is "the new normal"? It is a way in which cults are able to influence those they brainwash into accepting their teachings by making them seem prevalent, accepted and positive. For example, the idea of worshipping a man who claims to be God would be incredibly strange in everyday life. Within the closed environment of a cult, however, this behavior becomes "normal" to the extent that not doing it would seem strange to people within the cult! This process of persistent, social reinforcement is one of the most powerful ways in which the ideological brainwashing of cults is able to occur.

Think of cults as drug dealers. Perhaps the newcomer to the cult had been seeking something in their life and came across the cult, just as newcomers to the world of drugs often, misguidedly, seek out their first high of their own volition. The cult doesn't need to "push" the drug of their ideology onto the victim as the victim was already seeking the fulfillment of a void in their life. It is this initial "search" and "readiness" on the part of the people who are later brainwashed that makes them so susceptible to the brainwashing process itself.

Ideologies are another context, similar to cults, in which brainwashing is commonplace. The difference between a cult and an ideology is the focus of the ideology is on the idea itself rather than the person delivering the message and those who follow them. Whereas cults brainwash people into placing faith and trust in the cult leader and their followers, ideological brainwashing involves leading people to place absolute trust in an idea.

Ideological brainwashing is incredibly dangerous due to the fact it goes above and beyond any one individual. Think of extremist religious terrorism, for example. It is possible for a high profile figure within the ideology, such as Osama Bin Laden, to be killed. Does this kill support for the idea itself? No! The dead figures are praised as martyrs who gave their life to the ideology, thus increasing its attractiveness and allure to potential newcomers.

Almost any ideology is likely to have an extremist, fringe outskirt in which brainwashing takes place. Even something seemingly innocent like a pop band can have this impact. Young fans, at a psychologically impressionable age, link their sense of identity, happiness, and belonging to a pop group. They will gladly defend this group to extents that are unusually intense. Some pop groups have fans that even self-harm, using razor blades, if a member quits the group! If you carefully consider this phenomenon of the power of brainwashing even in accidental, innocent contexts, then consider how devastating the process can be in intended contexts like cults and terrorist groups.

Now that you have a clear understanding of the way brainwashing can occur in broader social contexts, such as cults and ideologies, it is important to understand that a personal, one-on-one context is also a ripe situation for elements of brainwashing to occur in. There are similarities and differences between "group" and "individual" brainwashing and understanding these nuances can help to identify when either type is occurring.

Personal brainwashing is similar to group brainwashing as it involves the slow and steady replacement of existing beliefs with new beliefs that serve the objectives of the brainwasher. Instead of relying on group dynamics to reinforce "the new normal," a one on one brainwashing situation will instead rely on a deep, personal connection between the brainwasher and the victim. This can be even more powerful than group brainwashing as the content can be modified and altered to the particular psychological constitution of the victim.

The Process of Brainwashing

Now that you understand the reality of what brainwashing is, and where it occurs, let's take a look at the specific process itself. Distinctions will be drawn between the way in which the process applies to both group and individual situations.

The starting point of any episode of brainwashing is the mental state and social circumstance of the victim. This is the foundation upon which the rest of the process is entirely reliant. Brainwashing is not something that can be carried out on absolutely anyone. It requires the identification of a person who is seeking something or trying to fill a void in their life.

So what kind of people are ideal victims for brainwashers? People who have had their existing reality shaken up by a recent event are prime targets for brainwashers. For example, many of the Western men who have travelled to become terrorists in Syria, and detonate suicide bombs, have done so after the death of a close friend or relative. When their existing world loses its meaning and certainty, brainwashers can step in and provide that certainty in the form of a murderous ideology.

Once a brainwashing victim has been identified, either in person or via the Internet, the actual process of brainwashing begins. Contrary to the popular image of a brainwasher as a wide-eyed psychopath who will incessantly and angrily indoctrinate their victim, real-world brainwashers are anything but this. They will come across as calm, friendly, rational people who have their lives together in a way the victim does not. Imagine being homeless and being befriended by a celebrity. This is how the process of meeting their brainwasher for the first time feels for a victim.

The brainwasher will often work initially on creating a level of trust and rapport between themselves and their victim. This usually involves creating both deep and superficial similarities. For example, superficial similarities may involve surface level preferences like an enjoyment of the same sport or even food! Deeper level rapport may involve some "deep" shared experience in the past of both the brainwasher and the victim. Brainwashers will convincingly fake these if needed. If the victim shares the fact that they have lost a relative in the past, guess what? The brainwasher suddenly has a similar story to tell.

The false emotional warmth and connection explained above is not the only aspect of brainwashing that occurs initially. The brainwasher will often provide gifts and other favors to their victim. For example, the brainwasher may treat them to meals or send them gadgets or other useful items. This creates a sense of gratitude and indebtedness from the victim to their brainwasher and softens up any resistance the victim may initially experience.

One of the most powerful examples of the above initial kindness can be taken from Prisoner of War camps. When American troops have been captured in the past, their captors often offer them American cigarettes and speak to them in a respectful way. This reverses the expectations of the victim and opens the victim's mind to the further brainwashing process that is to follow.

A utopian presentation is the next step in the brainwashing process, following the initial victim identification and rapport building stages. This involves the brainwasher slowly and increasingly offering a solution to all of the problems that the victim has opened up about. This is always done in a casual, offhand way at first to avoid any negative experiences of pressure the victim may experience otherwise. This utopian solution is always whatever cult, ideology or personality the brainwasher is trying to convert their victim to—terrorism, communism or just a charismatic brainwasher's own need for validation and praise.

When performed correctly, the initial stages of this process will leave a victim craving more and more information and understanding of the solution that is being hinted at. The brainwasher may even withhold this information initially, as if it is something that the victim must work at being worthy of attaining. This will lead to a strong motivation on behalf of the victim to seek out and accept the information they are eventually provided with. Thanks to the preceding steps, the poisonous ideas that are being implanted into the victim will seem as natural and refreshing as cold water on a hot day.

Once the victim is being spoon fed snippets of their new belief system, and responding well to them, the brainwasher will be very careful to reveal the right things at the right time. This is a concept that is sometimes known as "milk before meat" or "gradual revelation." It basically involves the presentation of easy to accept ideas before anything controversial is revealed. For example, in the case of religious terrorism, recruiters may initially focus on convincing their victim that God loves them. This is usually quite acceptable. More objectionable ideas, such as God wants you to blow yourself up, are saved until far further down the line. At this point, the brainwashing has reached the point of no return.

You may be questioning way a victim continues to engage with their brainwasher once the objectionable ideas begin to become apparent. The reason is threefold. First, the already vulnerable victim now feels a strong sense of liking and approval of their brainwasher.

Second, the victim has invested time and sometimes money into the process thus far. This is known as the "sunk cost fallacy." The victim is loath to "throw away all their hard work" by walking away from the process.

Finally, the brainwasher is likely to have amassed a lot of secretive and sensitive information on their victim. This "dirt" can then be held over the victim's head, either discreetly or overtly.

Both the ideas of a vulnerable victim and the "sunk cost fallacy" make logical sense. The idea of blackmail and control may be harder to understand at first. Why would a victim respond well to such threats? Well, they are rarely presented in a threatening way. For example, if the victim has divulged a lot of sensitive information to a brainwasher, and then begins to give signs of walking away, the brainwasher may appear concerned and insist that "if I can't help you anymore with your problems, I need to make sure someone else can. Perhaps your family or boss need to know what's been going on with you, so they can look out for you when I'm not there."

Because of the deep sense of rapport and warmth the brainwasher has manipulated their victim into feeling, the above form of blackmail and control is often actually perceived as kind, compassionate behavior. It is often enough to make the victim see "sense" and agree to remain on the brainwashing path they have embarked upon. Brainwashers are adept at making the pain and struggle of walking away seem epic, so staying becomes the preferable, easy option by default.

The end product of this process is the victim believing everything they have been indoctrinated to view as the truth. The power of the process is that the victim will feel they have chosen these views as their own and have sought them out through their own volition. This leaves a previously normal individual as an indoctrinated psychological slave to something they have no idea even exists.

The Impact of Brainwashing

The above analysis of the brainwashing process shows the severity and depth of the technique. It is inevitable that a process as powerful as this has lasting consequences. Some of the main impacts of brainwashing after the process has been completed will now be explored.

Loss of identity is one of the most serious side effects of brainwashing. A feature of many cults and ideologies is that people who complete their initiation process are given a new name. This allows the person's psyche to totally detach from their old identity. They can believe things and do things they would never have done before as the person they used to be no longer exists. When carried out carefully the brainwashing process leaves a victim feeling as if their old identity was no more real or permanent than a nightmare from which they have awoken.

So is brainwashing simply a process of ideas? Not at all. If brainwashing resulted in only the change of opinions then it would be far less of a problem than it actually is. The main danger of brainwashing is it not only changes the ways that people think and feel but also the way they behave. People go from functional members of the society with acceptable, positive jobs and interests to brainwashed zombies willing to carry out rape, murder, and suicide. This sounds sensational and dramatic, but it's true. Read on for the proof.

If you have any doubts about what brainwashing can drive a person to, consider the following examples. Members of some religious cults will gladly cut off all contact from their family, leave their careers behind, surrender all their wealth and possessions, and place their autonomy entirely in the hands of the organization that has brainwashed them. This is not all. The victim will see their new lifestyle as a blessing they are fortunate to have, rather than something unpleasant they have been forced into.

Another example of the toxic outcome of brainwashing is the repeated tale of young people becoming brainwashed by religious extremists to travel to a foreign land and drive a car packed full of explosives into a group of people they have never met and who have never hurt them. Such young victims are often educated people with a track record of success in life and a family history free of turmoil or abuse. These tragic losses of life are testament to the overwhelming, all-conquering power of the brainwashing process.

PTSD (post traumatic stress disorder) is another hallmark of those who manage to escape, or are rescued from, a situation of intense brainwashing. Brainwashing victims often show the same physical and psychological signs as war veterans who have witnessed their friends being blown apart next to them during combat. The severity of this traumatic aftermath shows that a brainwashing situation can harm a person as much as a world war.

Perhaps the most shocking examples of the long-term impact of brainwashing are the numerous instances of people who have been rescued or escaped from a brainwashing situation, only to later return of their own free will. Even once they are outside of the controlling, brainwashing environment, the legacy of the process runs so deep through a person's mind, they seek to return to it. This is a form of Stockholm syndrome. The escapees will actually praise their brainwashers far into the future and defend, support, and justify the ideological stances they were indoctrinated with while captive.

Chapter 8: The Dark Triad

What is The Dark Triad? - Understanding the Unholy Trinity

The Dark Triad is the key concept that ties together every other aspect of dark psychology. The name sounds like something from a movie, but it is a legitimate psychological concept recognized by all the top practitioners within the field. The Dark Triad is nothing more than the identification of the three most destructive and harmful psychological personality traits a person can have. This chapter will explain in detail what each of these traits are and the different ways they come across in practice. You are sure to recognize that The Dark Triad is the source from which all other dark psychology stems.

So what are the three traits that form the Triad? Machiavellianism, psychopathy, and narcissism. Many people may hear these terms and think they understand them instinctively. A psychopath is a dangerous murderer, right? A narcissist takes a few too many selfies? Wrong. Knowledge is power. Each of the concepts must be respected and understood for their power to become apparent.

To help your understanding of the powerful Dark Triad, an outline of each of its components, and what they consist of, will first be provided. Examples of how each dark psychology trait manifests in real-world situations will then be explored. This chapter offers a comprehensive insight into the theory, and the practice, of the three most significant and destructive concepts in the world of dark psychology.

What is Machiavellianism?

Machiavellianism draws its name from the political philosopher Machiavelli. In his classic work on political power and influence, "The Prince," Machiavelli outlines ideas, principles and tactics that have served as a blueprint for seekers of influence throughout history. So how exactly does a Machiavellian person come across?

The hallmarks of this Dark Triad trait are a willingness to focus on self-interest at all times, an understanding of the importance of image, perception and superficial appearance, and the ruthless exercise of power and cruelty over compassion and mercy.

In simple terms, Machiavellian people are incredibly strategic in their approach to life. The ramifications and consequences of any given action are thought out and assessed in terms of how they will impact upon the person carrying them out. The Machiavellian approach to the world can be summed up in a single question: "How will this action benefit me, and how will my public perception be impacted as a result?"

Machiavellian people are masters of doing whatever personally serves them while still managing to maintain a positive public image. To take but one example, think of former President Bill Clinton. He managed to behave according to his own sexual desires while still remaining "liked" among the general public. Contrast this with many other politicians who have succumbed to extra-marital temptation and are vilified in the public eye as a result.

Another example from the political arena is the public image of Barack Obama VS that of George W Bush. Ask around and most people will explain that Bush was a war president and Obama a president of peace. In actual fact, they are both about as militant as each other. Obama managed to manipulate his public perception to serve his own image while Bush did not. This is a powerful lesson on the idea of perception VS reality.

What is Psychopathy?

Psychopathy is hard to precisely define, but it refers to a psychological condition involving superficial charm, impulsivity, and a lack of commonly held "human" emotions such as empathy and remorse. Someone who exhibits enough of these traits is known as a psychopath. Psychopaths are some of the most dangerous people to walk the planet and are examples of wolves in sheep's clothing.

People might associate the word "psychopath" with the image of a machete wielding mad man wearing a mask. The reality is different and dangerous. True psychopaths are more likely to be the handsome, charming stranger who wins their victims over before ruining or even ending their life.

Interestingly, some of the top names in the field of business consistently score highly on psychopathy personality tests. Many people are beginning to see psychopathy as more of a problem for society than for the psychopaths' own lives. Psychopaths are often able to get to the top in any field they choose, be it finance or serial murder, because they are not constrained by the compassionate indecision that most human beings experience.

What is Narcissism?

A lot of people think of narcissism, and the narcissists who possess this trait, as people who simply "love themselves." This is along the right lines but not precise enough, especially when understanding narcissism through the lens of the dark triad. It is possible to have self-love without being a narcissist. So what are some of the distinctions between a person with high self-esteem and someone who is narcissistic to an extent that they are considered on the spectrum for The Dark Triad?

Someone who meets the medical diagnostic criteria for narcissism, to the point that they are considered to have a psychological disorder, is likely to exhibit a range of the following traits consistently. Narcissists are likely to have an excessively inflated self-worth, such as seeing their life as special and one of the most important in history, often the most important. Narcissists are not, in their own minds, only special—they are superior. They are a better species of person, higher in status than "normal" people. Their behavior reflects their sense of self-worth.

Some of the common outward manifestations of narcissism are an inability to accept criticism or dissent in any way. Similar to this need to be agreed with is the need to be flattered. Narcissists are in need of constant praise, approval and recognition and tend to organize their lives in a way that gives them constant access to others who fulfill this need.

The Dark Triad Applied

You now understand the concept of the Dark Triad, and the three psychological traits that form the basis of this fundamental area of dark psychology. It is important to not only understand the Triad itself but also the various ways in which it manifests in actual behavior. Some examples of behaviors will now be offered for each of the three Triad areas.

Machiavellian Actions

You know that a Machiavellian person is a political schemer concerned as much with their public image as they are with their cold-hearted pursuit of self-interest above all else. So how do Machiavellian people behave? This can be a hard thing to recognize as Machiavellian people are, by their nature, adept at hiding their true intentions and actions from public scrutiny. The following behaviors are all classic Machiavellian tactics that you are likely to encounter at one time or another.

For most people who do not meet the clinical definition of Machiavellianism, their public persona is usually a reflection of their genuine, private self. Everyone polishes their image and behavior a little in public but, by and large, most people's outward image is nothing more than a polished portrayal of who they really are.

Machiavellian people have a clear distinction between what they are and how they come across in the public eye. Examples help to illustrate this concept. There are many cases of serial murderers who have gotten away with their crimes for a long time because their outward image is so far apart from what people imagine a murderer to be. An example is a religious leader who spends a lot of time on charity work and seeming to help regular people while actually committing horrific acts of violence and sexual assault in their spare time. Their public actions are the "mask" that hides their private self from scrutiny for such a long time.

Examples of such a distinction between intent and appearance can be found in areas less extreme than serial murder. There are countless tales of leaders in the world of business who manage to ruthlessly cut jobs and pursue profit over people whenever possible. The very best of these bosses, in terms of Machiavellianism, are actually able to get people to buy into the notion that they are behaving through necessity or even compassion! Such leaders are almost role models for those who wish to serve only their own desires while seeming to be a "man of the people" at the same time.

A willingness to exploit people is another hallmark of Machiavellian individuals. To illustrate this example, think of a newcomer to an average office workplace. If this person was not clinically Machiavellian they would look around and see a room full of different coworkers to get to know. Each a human being, just like them. Some good people, some bad people.

A Machiavellian office newcomer would see every single colleague, boss or team member as just a resource or piece of a puzzle to use and exploit. Rather than seeing others as fellow human beings, the Machiavellian individual would just see a series of strategic threats and weaknesses to manage, exploit or neutralize. This is a large part of the reason that Machiavellian people are so aware of how they come across. They know this outward portrayal is the key to exerting influence and successfully exploiting everyone they come across.

One of the original Machiavellian principles, derived from "The Prince," is an insistence on only keeping a word or promise if it serves self-interest to do so. At first glance, this idea might lead to an understanding of Machiavellian people as those who are known as untrustworthy. This is a fundamental misunderstanding. If a Machiavellian person breaks their word, they do so in a way which actually makes them appear noble and somehow praiseworthy. This can be illustrated with an example drawn from contemporary politics. Do you remember, prior to Barack Obama's election, his promise to close down Guantanamo Bay? Has this been kept? No. Instead, Obama somehow has portrayed himself as a "noble man held back by a cruel system" rather than a "politician who broke his word." This is the fundamental difference between a skilled Machiavellian man and a regular person who can't be trusted.

The instilling of fear in the people around them is another hallmark of Machiavellian individuals. This stems directly from "The Prince," which urges people to be both feared and loved simultaneously. If this is not possible, then the book states being feared is preferable to being loved. This concept of the desirability of being loved and feared at the same time relates directly to the Machiavellian trait of splitting a public and private perception. The perfect

Machiavellian is able to inspire fear and obedience in the very people who would genuinely claim to feel love stronger than fear as a result.

Psychopathic Actions

You have a clear understanding of the main psychopathic traits and what differentiates true psychopaths from those in the public imagining. Unless you are a trained psychotherapist with intimate access to a person you will not be able to recognize them as a psychopath on the basis of theoretical knowledge. Instead, it is essential to recognize the outward manifestations of psychopathy, as these are usually the only way to detect psychopathy before it is too late.

Charm is one of the most common outward behaviors of a psychopathic person. It must be understood, however, that this is superficial charm rather than deep, genuine charm. If you think about a genuinely charming person from your lifetime you are likely to recognize they had positive personality traits underpinning outward displays of behavior. If such a genuinely charming person behaved in a charming way it was a genuine expression of kindness and a desire to make people happy. This is not the case with a psychopath.

Psychopaths are able to exhibit all the outward signs of charm such as physical attractiveness, apparent warmth, and interest in others. The inward motivation behind such outward displays is the reason it is such a red flag. Psychopaths view charm as very much part of an equation. The internal reasoning goes something like "If I display signs of charm to this person it will make them feel this way and I will experience this advantage as a result." Everything is very calculated and shallow—there is no genuine depth of feeling behind any outward displays of behavior.

Lying is another trademark feature of psychopaths. It is not, on its own, enough to place a person within the diagnostic category of psychopathy. When combined with other traits, however, it can indicate a psychopathic personality. Lying comes as naturally for a psychopath as breathing does for most psychologically healthy people. A psychopath is able to convincingly present the truth as whatever they need it to be in a particular moment. Psychopaths also don't show outward signs of lying as they have no emotional attachment or feelings of shame, guilt, or excitement about their lies. For psychopaths, lying is just "doing what is needed at the time."

A lack of remorse is another distinctive feature that separates psychopaths from non-psychopathic individuals. Many people who have committed atrocious acts, such as murder, feel a deep sense of guilt and shame about what they have done and even take their own life due to these feelings. It's not that psychopaths choose not to be remorseful—they are physically incapable of it. Asking a psychopath to feel remorse is like asking a deaf person to listen to music.

Closely linked to a lack of remorse is a lack of guilt. Humans typically feel guilt when they have broken some kind of moral norm that they personally value. As psychopaths do not think in terms of right and wrong, only useful or not useful, guilt is an alien concept to them. The closest thing a psychopath might express to guilt or remorse is a regret that they did not carry out their psychopathic deeds to their own high standards.

A lack of impulse control is another signature aspect of psychopathy. Most people have internal controls and mechanisms that prevent them from behaving rashly. A psychopath lacks these prevention mechanisms. If a psychopath sees an opportunity they wish to exploit they act without hesitation or a second thought. This could involve killing someone they wish to kill, raping someone they wish to rape, or stealing something they wish to steal. This ruthless impulsivity is what makes psychopaths some of the most effective people in fields such as the military and world of business. The automatic taking of decisive action is a trait many non-psychopaths lack, and this lack actually is a detriment to progress in life.

Empathy is a human ability to experience pain on behalf of another. Psychopaths are utterly incapable of empathy of any kind. Other human beings are no more real to psychopaths than are stick figures crudely drawn on paper. Their lives have no value or meaning outside of what they can provide to the psychopathic person. If a psychopath sees something bad happen to someone their reaction is to think "How does this affect me? How can I use this to my advantage?" rather than any kind of heartfelt reaction at all.

Narcissistic Actions

One of the earliest signs of a narcissist is fantasies and imaginings of immense levels of power and status. Many narcissists report childhood fantasies of being worshipped and adored. While many non-narcissistic people may have the occasional daydream of power and status, a narcissist will strongly feel they deserve this praise and elevation as a basic right. The fact they are not being worshipped and revered at all times is a personal affront to the psychological outlook of a psychopath.

The belief that "I am better than most people. They are not worthy of me. I am above them" is a commonly held view of serious narcissists. Most people experience fluctuations in self-image as a result of their achievements and behaviors in life. This is not the case with narcissists. Narcissists view flattery and praise as something that they should automatically receive, at all times, regardless of any change in circumstances.

The inflated sense of self-worth that narcissists experience internally has implications on their outward reality as well. This typically manifests in two ways—the need for agreement and praise and the hatred of criticism or rejection. Praise and agreement are like oxygen for the narcissistic ego, whereas criticism and dissent are like poison.

To understand what narcissism looks like when taken to its logical conclusion, picture a dictator in a hermit state. Such people demand worship from those they have power over, the building of statues in their likeness and complete obedience and acceptance. Any act of dissent or disagreement is met with swift and brutal punishment. North Korea would be a perfect modern example of the extreme manifestation of narcissism. The rulers of that nation demand to be revered like Gods and execute and torture anyone who even dares to express a thought or idea which isn't completely in line with official state doctrine.

Sadism

Sadism is a shocking but necessary footnote to the Dark Triad chapter. Modern psychological researchers have proposed that the dark triad is, in actual fact, a dark tetrad with sadistic personality disorder offering the fourth pillar. Sadism is perhaps the hardest dark personality trait to understand as it is the least relatable for many people.

Almost everyone has an aspect of their personality, or background, in which they can recognize signs of Machiavellianism, psychopathy and narcissism to an extent. Sadism is alien to most people though as they cannot even rationally understand the basis for it.

Sadism is defined as the deriving of pleasure from the suffering of others. This adds a worrying dimension to the preexisting Dark Triad traits. If, for example, a Machiavellian leader caused others to suffer, they would not regret it, but would also not enjoy the suffering. It would be viewed dispassionately. Add sadism into the mix, however, and the worrying occurrence of pleasure, even sexual pleasure, being derived from brutal acts occurs.

The defining feature that sets sadism apart from other aspects of dark psychology is the fact it involves cruelty for no purpose other than pleasure. It is not to serve a larger aim or due to some inherent lack of control. Sadists seek out the suffering of others purely for entertainment, in the same way regular people might watch a sports contest.

Chapter 9: Dark Psychological Seduction

The Devil's Desire

Seduction and sexual conquest are such common motives and features of dark psychology that they deserve their own chapter. Almost everyone has a friend who has been seduced by someone using dark psychological principles. Perhaps in your own efforts in the dating world you have tried to use some form of underhand influence to your own advantage.

The human sex drive is one of the most powerful urges and an inability to fulfill it can lead to great stress, worry, and unhappiness in a person's life. Conversely, some of the most famous historical figures are known for the frequent and full fulfillment of their sexual urges. Kings and emperors have often been afforded the finest women in the world as a reward for their elevated social status.

One particularly famous example of a powerful seducer is King Henry the 8th of England. His appetite for women was so strong he created a new religious movement in order to allow him to marry as many women as he chose. He also exercised utter control over his wives, with many of them ending up beheaded.

King Henry the 8th is but one historical example of the role of seduction and desire within the world of dark psychology. The prevalence of this particular topic and motivation is a sign that it forms a key aspect of dark psychology. A failure to understand how seduction and desire relate to dark psychology leaves a student with an incomplete knowledge of the topic.

So is all seduction dark psychological seduction? No. All seduction involves the pursual of another human being. Most people who are not adept at the skills of dark psychological manipulators do this in a very clumsy and unstructured way. To illustrate this idea, think of the classic romantic comedy setup with a clumsy guy making mistake after mistake in his pursuit of the girl. A skilled psychological seducer is more like Ryan Gosling in Crazy, Stupid Love, or Will Smith in Hitch. They know what they want and know how to get it.

As you will see in this chapter, the use of dark psychology in the pursuit of seduction is neither inherently good nor bad. This can only be judged in relation to the impact it has on the person seduced. An entire section of this chapter is dedicated to understanding the difference in outcome between moral and immoral seduction.

So how can this chapter be used? At the very least, it will complete your understanding of dark psychology as a general concept. Any book not containing detail on seduction would be an incomplete work. You can also make practical use of the information you desire. Whether you choose to protect yourself and your loved ones from dark seducers, or become one yourself, is entirely your choice.

This chapter will change the way you see the dating world forever.

Why Dark Psychological Seduction?

One of the main questions people often have when they come across the idea of dark psychological seduction for the first time is "why?" Why do people choose this particular path of attraction? Is it not better to go on dates and court someone slowly and honestly? Understanding why people choose the path of dark seduction is the first step in understanding its immense power.

Let's consider someone who goes about their love life without using any ideas or techniques found in the world of dark psychology. This person will be referred to as a "conventional dater." This conventional dater spends a lot of time and money on someone before they ever enjoy them sexually. They may marry them and make a public promise of faithfulness and commitment no matter what.

Later down the line, the conventional dater, now the conventional spouse, may find that their life is not as they imagined. Both they and their partner rushed into the wedding and it has not filled the expectations they had for it. Both partners are left with a choice. Either stay in a lifeless and unsatisfactory marriage or cheat on their spouse. Who would want either path?

This unhappy conventional data can be contrasted with the satisfied seducer who uses dark psychology to get whatever they want out of the area of romance. No other person is too important to them because they know their use of dark psychology means they will always be able to find someone else. This makes them approach life with a carefree, non-needy mindset.

If a satisfied seducer does choose to settle down eventually, they do so without any feeling of "settling" or rushing into the first relationship they have haphazardly stumbled across. This actually leads to a happier, more contented marriage as it is entered into from a place of abundance rather than scarcity.

So how can a satisfied seducer have so much success and influence within the dating world? It is due to the power of the principles they understand, and the skill they have in executing the techniques that stem from the principles. Throughout this book you have seen countless examples of how dark psychology can work in many areas of life. Why would the world of dating and seduction be any different?

One of the key advantages that users of dark psychology have over their rivals is that their understanding of the human mind is almost like a secret weapon. If a conventional data is a clumsy guy stumbling blindly through the world of romance, accepting whatever happens to come his way, the skilled seducer is a sniper, hunting and enjoying whatever they happen to crave at the time.

Someone who tries out the principles of dark psychology within the dating world is likely to be amazed at how their experiences differs from their past efforts. A feeling of control and confidence replaces a past one of doubt, neediness and insecurity. Amazingly, the dark psychology user will not only find that they feel better about their own results, they will also see that the people they are interacting with are enjoying the experience a lot more as well. This is because dark psychology teaches a seducer exactly what people are looking for within the romantic world and also teaches the seducer how to provide it.

Many people who have applied their dark psychological knowledge to the world of dating and seduction for the first time describe it as a eureka moment. Use of these techniques and ideas gives them the ability to finally get what they want from life and fulfill their deepest, longest held desires in the process.

Is Dark Seduction Evil?

One of the most common queries newcomers to the concept of dark psychological seduction have is whether the techniques are immoral or evil in some way. Like almost anything, dark psychological seduction is neither inherently good nor bad. The way it is used determines the extent to which it can be judged morally. Broadly speaking, people use dark psychological seduction with one of three primary motivations—to help the people they seduce, to hurt the people they seduce or to only help themselves.

Many people find it hard to believe that anyone would go into the world of dark psychological seduction with the intent of helping the other person. Surely all seducers are selfish and careless, right? Wrong.

One of the most famous ideas from the world of seduction is "leave them better than you found them." People who hold this viewpoint feel that there is no need for someone to "lose" in the process of seduction. Both parties, the seducer and the person being seduced, can enjoy a "win/win" experience where no one loses out.

So how does a person enjoy a seductive lifestyle while making sure they leave people better than they found them? Never lying or misleading a victim outright is a key idea behind ethical seduction. One of the most common hallmarks of insincere people is "leading on" by promising the world and delivering nothing. Skilled seducers do not make promises they cannot keep. Rather, they simply allow the person they are seducing to get caught up in the moment and enjoy the experience fully.

Other individuals enter the world of dark psychological destruction with less pure motives. Their care is to only satisfy their own needs and desires and they will gladly mislead, hurt or harm the person they are seducing. Such uncaring narcissism is paradoxically attractive to some people who, bizarrely, return to patterns of being used time and time again.

The behavior of someone who goes about their psychological seduction without a care other than their own satisfaction often ends up causing them problems. If people go into the world of seduction without a totally carefree, nihilistic attitude, problems can arise. This type of seducer often ends up in a situation of having unwanted children and having to pay a lot of child support. They are also more likely to invoke the fury of scorned conquests they have carelessly discarded. People who are too cavalier in their seductive efforts have even been murdered by jealous or hurt former lovers.

Two major approaches to dark psychological seduction have now been explored—those who aim to help others, and those who aim to hurt others. We will now examine the third approach—the person who thinks only of their own experience.

Someone who uses dark psychological seduction as a technique that only matters to their own life and its outcomes is likely to see the process of seduction as "self-development on steroids." Going against the human instinct to stay in the zone of comfort and familiarity, and instead pushing the boundaries of what is possible in the dating world forces someone to discover their own strengths and weaknesses in a brutal way.

Such people as just described are more likely to derive enjoyment from their exploration and manipulation of social rules and conventions as they are from the romance they manage to attain. This type of path is similar to the one walked by someone who goes from obese to healthy through a focused series of effort and self betterment. The impact they have upon the people they are seducing is less important to them than the impact their dark seduction has on themselves.

The Starting Point of Seduction

You now know the basic concept of dark psychological seduction and the reasons people choose to use it. You also are aware that such people can be good, bad or indifferent. So now the motive and intention of dark psychological seducers are clear, how exactly do they do what they do?

Most seducers are likely to have a "guiding approach" that underpins their efforts as well as specific tactics that stem from this philosophy. In our exploration of these different philosophies we will see many familiar ideas from dark psychology. Seduction is often the area in which psychological ideas are moved from abstract theory into applied practice.

One approach to dark psychological seduction is the deployment of a very structured, rigid process. Such seducers feel that they have mapped out the sequence of attraction to an almost flowchart-like level of precision and detail. They see the process of psychological seduction as predictable and replicable. Their systems are likely to work for them in particular but also others in general who are able to understand and implement them properly.

A hallmark of such seducers is their usage of a series of different stages. Some will try and lead their target through a structured range of emotions—such as interest, followed by attraction followed by excitement. Such seducers see their seduction process as a series of checkpoints to pass through in order to achieve their eventual aim.

One of the strengths of a structured system of seduction is it gives those who follow it a feeling of certainty that they always know what to do next. They don't have to worry about what to do next, because the process is as habitual and routine as driving a car or brushing teeth. A disadvantage to this rigid approach is that it can cause problems when someone is not responding as intended. Structured seducers sometimes lose sight of the fact that people are unpredictable individual humans rather than predictable computer operating systems.

The approach to seduction that stands most strongly in contrast to the structured approach is the "natural" approach. This involves cultivating genuine emotional states internal to the seducer and then freely expressing them to the person they wish to seduce. For example, a person using this type of unstructured seduction is likely to spend time understanding their own emotional makeup and outlook and how to perfect it. They then express this externally to other people. The basic philosophy behind this approach is "I can't make other people feel good until I feel good."

NLP and hypnotic seduction is a subset of dark psychological seduction and the ideas that underpin the general concept. Unlike structured seduction, or the more natural variant, NLP/hypnotic seduction involves triggering particular emotional states in the person who is the target of seduction and then linking these states to the hypnotic seducer.

For example, the NLP approach to seduction may involve allowing a person to explore their own intense positive emotions and then "anchoring" the trigger for these emotions to the person who induced them, the seducer. The seducer is then able to trigger intense physical pleasure in their victim by issuing the anchor, such as a particular gesture of tone or voice.

Hypnotic seduction is a difficult technique to use regularly. This is because few things put someone's guard up as much as the slightly odd techniques involved in NLP. Structured or unstructured seduction at least comes across as "normal," whereas hypnotic seduction does not. Some people respond very well to it, however, and those who do are likely to be a better match in terms of personal compatibility with the hypnotic seducer.

Some psychological seducers are able to invert the traditional seduction dynamics and gender roles to great effect. For example, the typical view of seduction, throughout history, is that the man is the aggressive party and the woman plays the more passive role. Inverting this can lead to powerful outcomes. Some men find that they are able to allow themselves to become the prize, the one who is chased. This inversion of the expected norm can lead to a refreshing change from the mundane routine of dating for everyone involved.

Female psychological seducers are also able to use the inversion of traditional seduction dynamics to powerful effect. Some men are totally overwhelmed if the woman is the aggressive, confident pursuer and a lot of women also report feeling a sense of empowerment and proactivity that they have not experienced within their romantic life at any time before.

Some people also enter the world of psychological seduction with the intention of breaking free from the constraints of monogamy that have held them back throughout their life. This approach is sometimes known as polyamory, an open relationship or some other variation on this theme depending on the need of the person pursuing it. By learning dark psychological techniques, this type of seducer is able to pursue their true desires in a way that is open, honest, and effective.

The Techniques

You now know the "guiding principles" behind psychological approaches to seduction and the motivations that people have for carrying them out. So how exactly do people go about translating these ideas and theories into actionable principles and techniques?

The "indirect approach" is a key technique within the world of seduction. One mistake that many people make in the world of conventional dating is offering a cheesy and unappealing icebreaker when introducing themselves to a potential seduction target.

"Nice eyes." "You look pretty." "Good song, right?" All these are examples of some of the most clichéd icebreakers out there. Why are these so bad? Women are likely to have heard them countless times before and are instantly switched off upon hearing them. When a seducer uses such an awful line it suggests they are a bland and unappealing person.

The indirect opener is a breath of fresh air in comparison to its clichéd precedents. An indirect opener is any icebreaking gambit that initiates a social interaction without conveying sexual intent. This is often posed in the form of an "intriguing question." For example, a seducer using an indirect opener might ask "Settle this for me or my buddies over there—do men or women lie more?" This sparks a conversation and shows the seducer to be an interesting person who is looking for nothing more than a good conversation.

Indirect openers also have the advantage of eliminating the possibility of rejection. Someone using an indirect opener is not "offering" themselves in any way to the person they wish to seduce and it is impossible to "reject" something or someone that has not been "offered."

Social proof is another key technique in the world of dark psychological seduction. People who are popular are instantly more attractive than those who are not. Why? It's human extinct to assume that if a person is widely liked, there is something likable about them. Anyone's worst nightmare is being seduced by some creepy loner with no friends and no one they are close to. A person like this is likely to be better lonely and needy.

So how can social proof be used in the area of psychological seduction? This is a case where "showing is more powerful than telling." Many people make the mistake of actually talking about their popularity or success in a way that comes across as bragging or some other form of try hard, unnatural behavior. It is better to simply be at a table in a club or bar with a group of interesting people. This conveys social value without rubbing it in a person's face.

One use of social proof is particularly devious. Let's picture a psychological seducer in a bar or club environment. They see a girl they want to go and talk to. Instead of directly approaching the person they wish to seduce, they instead approach someone else first, strike up a conversation with them, move over to their original target and begin interacting with the originally intended person. This removes the perception of loneliness that would otherwise exist. It can also spark a little jealous rivalry between the two women!

Being something of a challenge is a dark psychological technique outside of the grasp of most conventional daters. Most people make the mistake of being too keen, too eager, and too available. An example would be a man who calmly waits while some girl in a bar ignores him completely or a woman who puts up with some form of disloyal or disrespectful behavior from the person they are with. The opposite of this display of low personal standards is a display of being "challenging." This can take numerous forms.

One technique that makes use of the "challenging" principle is to walk away from a seduction target if needed. For example, if the target is being cheeky or sassy, the seducer can playfully say "you're done" and turn to walk away. Most times, the target will be wowed by this unconventional behavior and enjoy interacting with a person who has standards and self-confidence.

Another way of being challenging is by using carefully chosen, playful teases during the course of an interaction. Most people, when trying to seduce someone, are excessively positive. They offer compliment after compliment, laugh at all the jokes they hear and generally do everything to imprison their own perception within the confines of "nice but bland." By throwing out a playful tease, the seducer offers a fun emotional "spike" which draws in the person they wish to seduce.

One of the main motivations behind human experience is to seek out that which is new and exciting. This is particularly true within the world of romance where most people are looking for something fun and exciting. There is a reason that clichéd lines and dating profiles are such a universal punch line—because they are boring and don't actually work. An antidote to the disease of blandness is learning how to stand out in a good way.

The concept of standing out in a good way can be put into practice by first considering what everyone else is doing wrong. Once this is clear, the seducer should consider how these wrong actions would make the seduction target feel. Once this is understood, the seducer can put the pieces together to answer the question of "How can I do things differently from everyone else in a way that would make the other person respond well?"

Some of the most common ways of standing out in a good way include dressing a little better or a little more interestingly than other people in the venue. For example, if a place is very casual, dressing up very slightly can be a huge advantage. No one is suggesting you wear a tuxedo to a sports bar, but making a little extra effort can be very powerful indeed.

Establishing a frame of leading is another useful technique in the world of psychological seduction. Most people are happy to be led. Indecisiveness is one of the least attractive qualities in a human being. Ways of showing decisiveness and the ability to lead include physically moving around a venue, suggesting a change of venue, and not being afraid to disagree with something that is said. Many people, men in particular, make the mistake of behaving contrary to this principle by being an indecisive leaf in the wind rather than a strong, confident alpha male who knows that they want in life.

A natural extension of knowing how to lead is knowing how to close. Spend some time talking to the women in your life and they are likely to share many stories of men who were wishy-washy and indecisive when it was time for the first kiss, first sexual encounter, or some other romantic milestone. Hesitation on the part of a woman can also be off-putting for men. Think about it. Who wants to be with someone who doesn't even know what they want? Decisiveness and the ability to take action are key components in ensuring a psychological seduction goes as intended.

Some psychological seducers are actually able to harness dark psychological traits such as elements of psychopathy in pursuit of their romantic aims. One of the trademark features of a psychopath is an ability to not feel fear when interacting with other people. Most men and women are paralyzed by fear and, specifically, the fear of rejection from someone they are romantically interested in. A specific technique exists that can be learned from the example of fearless psychopaths and used to overcome this fear.

So how exactly does a person overcome their fear of rejection? Simple. By being rejected time and time again and realizing it is not actually that bad. Over time, psychological seducers learn that it is always better to be the person who tried and failed than the person who didn't have the confidence to try. Taking action becomes its own reward and the seducer loses their nervousness and hesitation in the process.

People who put this desensitization to rejection technique into action will start to realize that the less they fear rejection, the less it actually occurs. Being confident and calm when interacting with new people is one of the byproducts of this method. The more a person gets rejected initially, the less they will fear future rejection. This translates into actual success and less rejection in the long run! Try it and see.

Chapter 10: Case Studies

You now know the main ideas behind dark psychology and the way these ideas are applied in a variety of situations. This is powerful, but, on its own, not enough. By taking the time to learn about dark psychology through the analysis of real world case studies, you will see the ideas in this book brought to life.

The case studies are also eye opening, fascinating tales in their own right. They offer an insight into some of the most psychologically rare types of people this planet has ever produced.

Each case study is laid out in a way that is as useful as possible for a budding disciple of dark psychology. Factual information relating to each case study is provided before psychological insight is extracted and simplified. Each case study will then be directly linked back to the dark psychology found in this book to allow you to understand it in a richer and more meaningful way.

The cases contained in this chapter are the most extreme examples of dark psychology throughout human history. They are presented not to be glorified, or even judged, but instead learned from.

The Final Testimony of Ted Bundy

Facts

Ted Bundy was one of the most notorious serial killers in the history of the world. His story is that of a textbook psychopathic killer in many ways. One fascinating aspect of Ted Bundy's story is the amount of material published on him and his crimes, due to their high profile, and Bundy's willingness to give interviews and offer insights. With many such high-profile criminals, the level of hype and intrigue surrounding them often outweighs the actual gravity of their crimes. This is not the case with Bundy.

No confirmed total of murders has been definitively linked to Ted Bundy. He was charged with 30 but has frequently hinted the total could be close to 100. No one knows for sure, and many analysts have speculated that Bundy himself had no idea of how many victims he killed.

Due to the time Bundy spent on death row after being sentenced to death, a lot of material was produced related to Bundy's psychology, background, and possible motivation behind his crimes. In addition to this, a lot of posthumous analysis has taken place that has sought to dispassionately examine the crimes, and the man who carried them out, in an effort to understand one of the most extreme murderers to ever be caught.

There are many details related to Bundy's crimes that have gone on to be understood as absolutely textbook in the world of psychopathic serial killers, their motivations, and their methods. We will now explore some of the more striking aspects of Bundy's crimes before analyzing this man and his life for insights into this book's chosen dark psychological principles.

One standout feature of Bundy's lengthy murder career is the way it evolved over time. Bundy himself stated that when he first started killing he was sloppy and opportunistic. Chillingly, like other masters of their field, Bundy evolved his process over time and became more elaborate, careful, and methodological in the way he operated.

It is hard to have a definitive insight into the mind of Bundy because the man was known for disguising the truth as much as possible. He was frequently described as a "changeling" or "shapeshifter" due to this ability to mask his true physical appearance with subtle but comprehensive misdirections, as well as his ability to offer whichever biographical red herring happened to serve his own purpose at the time.

As skillfully as Bundy was able to conceal his true motivation, method, and background, his deceptive ways provided invaluable insight into the nature of deceptive, psychopathic killers. The main lessons related to the dark psychology of Ted Bundy will now be summarized.

Insights & Links to Dark Psychology

Many books have been published aiming to understand and learn from the case study of Ted Bundy. Instead of spending hours laboring through such works, you can read the main insights that are concisely offered in this book to boost your understanding of dark psychological topics.

Deception is one of the dark psychological traits that Bundy was a master of. This extended to his way of interacting with people both during and following his crime spree. Bundy was able to deceive both physically and psychologically.

Bundy clearly understood the power of perception and public image. It is an undisputed fact that many people who encountered him found him to be a charming and attractive man. This is a hallmark of psychopaths who are able to project the outward appearance of charm and desirability without any inner truth to that facade. The emotional coldness and detachment of men like Bundy become clear when you stop and consider that a human being was able to inspire attraction and comfort in his victims moments before brutally assaulting and killing them in some of the most sadistic and ritualistic crimes known to humanity.

Psychopaths' ability to understand the motivations and biases of those they manipulate is also apparent in Bundy's actions and words. Nothing illustrates this better than the interview Bundy gave to moral campaigner James Dobson the night before his execution. Knowing full well that Dobson was campaigning against pornography at the time, Bundy was able to portray his motivation as stemming entirely from early exposure to pornography. He also skillfully fed Dobson exactly what he wanted to hear in a bid to deflect attention from his actual actions, alluding to demonic possession and other material that was sure to catch the attention of Dobson's Christian audience.

Bundy also illustrated a psychopath's ability to detach entirely from what they are doing. He was notorious for using cryptic hints regarding the location of bodies in exchange for more time before his execution. In the mind of a psychopath such as Bundy, a dead child's body is nothing more than a bargaining chip to be exploited for personal gain.

The high intelligence of many psychopaths is also evidenced by the way Bundy operated. The reason he was able to remain at large for so long was due to his in-depth knowledge of law enforcement detection methods, in an era where such things were less widely known than they are today. Bundy also showed strong signs of sadism and narcissism by torturing his victims, taking pictures of their bodies, and referring to himself in the third person.

Lessons From History's Narcissistic Dictators

Facts

One of the textbook traits of narcissists is their view of their own status and self-worth as far in excess of anything actually justified by reality. This usually leads to people with an inflated ego being trapped in lifestyles and situations that they see as fundamentally beneath them. Occasionally, someone with a narcissistic personality is born into a situation where they have the power and status to express their narcissism fully. Nothing exemplifies this more than some of history's dictators who had the power and control to match their egos. Some of their stories are presented here.

Saparmurat Niyazov is one of the best examples of a narcissist having the opportunity to fulfill grandiose inclinations. He took over as leader of Turkmenistan and was able to take advantage of a power vacuum left by the collapse of Soviet ideology. His ascent from leader to pure manifestation of narcissism began when he decided he should be President for Life of Turkmenistan. From there, total power led to some memorably narcissistic choices.

One of the more infamous aspects of Niyazov's rule was the renaming of the months of the year to reflect his own personal glory. He implemented bizarrely specific laws in accordance with his personal whims, such as restricting citizens' appearance and renaming common everyday objects according to what he felt they should be called.

Perhaps the most powerful example of Niyazov's grandiosity was his production of a religious text that was given equal status within the country as established scriptures such as The Holy Qur'an. Other dictators, such as Colonel Gaddafi of Libya, have produced similarly "revered" texts. This is a known trait perhaps best evidenced by the status afforded to Adolf Hitler's "Mein Kampf" within Nazi Germany.

A better-known, yet equally terrifying, dynasty of dictators is that of the leaders of North Korea. Current dictator Kim Jong Un and his Father Kim Jong Il are afforded the status of deities within their tightly controlled nation and this is reflected in the "facts" that North Korean citizens are provided about their lives. For example, Kim Jong Il is remembered for shooting a round of golf consisting of all "holes in one" at his first attempt at the sport. North Korean citizens are so tightly indoctrinated into the political personality cult that governs their lives that they often take such claims at face value.

Insights & Links to Dark Psychology

So what can such outlandish examples teach us about narcissism? Many of the traits exhibited by such dictators are examples of how controlling and pedantic narcissists become when granted enough power to carry out their wishes.

Let's take North Korea as an example. The current dictator, Kim Jong Un, is reported to have had his own uncle executed for yawning in a meeting. The method of execution? An anti-aircraft weapon capable of destroying fighter jets. This is an example of the narcissist's need for flattery and anger when not receiving it taken to its logical conclusion.

The many instances of dictators producing religious, spiritual, or philosophical treatises which are then elevated to the status of required, sanctified reading within the country is an illustration of the narcissistic concept of being "special" and "equal to humanity's greatest figures." In narcissists' minds, they are the contemporaries of prophets and saints, a truly rare breed. If you can grasp the extent to which they truly believe this to be the case, then their publication of such egotistical texts begins to make a twisted kind of sense.

Hitler - The Modern Machiavelli

Facts

Many parallels can be drawn between the political ideas of Machiavelli, as expressed through "The Prince," and the political career of Adolf Hitler. The argument can therefore be made that Hitler is the best possible illustration of what a true modern Machiavellian leader looks like. We will first take a look at the similarities between Hitler's thoughts and deeds and those of Machiavelli, before exploring the insights into Machiavellianism as a trait that Hitler provides.

One of the first similarities that can be drawn between Machiavelli and Hitler is the assertion in "The Prince" that peace should only been seen as a brief respite in a never-ending war. Hitler was devoted to conquest and planned to eventually take over the entire world under his totalitarian Third Reich. Hitler is therefore the closest thing the modern world has seen to Machiavelli's idea of a ceaseless warrior ruler.

Machiavelli was also an advocate of creating and manipulating reality to sort a predetermined political aim. Infamously, one of Hitler's core doctrines was the persecution and subsequent extermination of Germany's Jewish population. One of the key events that helped Hitler pursue this genocidal goal was the false flag operation known as the Reichstag Fire.

It is a matter of debate whether Hitler engineered this event to suit his anti-Jewish and anti-Communist agenda, but a large body of evidence suggests he did exactly that. Regardless of the exact circumstance, the incident is a powerful illustration of a Machiavellian false flag tactic being used to serve another aim entirely.

One of the key ideas behind Machiavelli's political thought, and subsequent Machiavellian individuals, is that power is a worthy end goal in and of itself. No matter what methods are used to hold on to and retain power, they are justified according to Machiavelli's blueprint of how a leader should behave.

Hitler is a textbook example of this concept in action. Hitler knew how to manipulate the political system of the time as well as the hearts and minds of the German people. There is a strong suggestion that Hitler may have escaped Nazi Germany and fled to Argentina to live out the rest of his days surrounded by fellow Nazi escapees. This is difficult to prove either way but is a plausible illustration of never letting go of power, even in the face of apparent death.

Perhaps the most significant and apparent link between Hitler and Machiavelli is the concept of "it is better to be loved and feared, but if that is not possible, feared rather than loved." It is easy to overlook the kind of devotion, love, and even worship that Hitler was able to inspire in the German people of the era. History since World War Two has painted Hitler as the epitome and embodiment of evil, the closest thing the Earth has ever seen to an incarnation of Satan. At the time, though, Hitler was equally adept at triggering responses of love and fear. One needs only to watch video of Hitler's speeches to show the mixture of awe and terror Hitler was able to provoke.

Insights & Links to Dark Psychology

One of the key Machiavellian ideas to emerge from "The Prince" is the principle of not keeping your word, your promise, if it is not in your interest to do so. Machiavelli emphasizes the need to at least appear to be truthful, no matter what the reality of the situation may be.

Hitler offers a true insight into how real-world figures with political power are able to carry out this concept. One trademark feature of Hitler's speeches was that they delivered epic and hard-to-implement promises that would never realistically reach fruition. Although Hitler was not able to deliver on the ideas he put forward in his rhetoric, he managed to maintain the image of being a man striving to deliver on his word. This is a clear real-world example of the Machiavellian theory of separating truth and public perception to powerful psychological effect.

Another Machiavellian idea exemplified by Hitler was the consolidation of power and the elimination of threats. Hitler systematically eliminated anyone who opposed his quest to lead Germany back to its former glory. He eliminated absolutely anyone who stood in his way—former allies, holders of rival ideologies or ethnic groups Hitler felt the need to rid Germany of. This concentration of power led to Hitler being able to exercise as much influence as he did. This shows that Machiavellian theory is in fact effective in practice, even in the modern era.

A final insight provided by Hitler into the world of dark psychology is his use of, and enthusiasm for, sadism. This quarter of the Dark Tetrad is especially apparent in the way Hitler treated those forced into his concentration camps. The fates of these poor souls included torture, medical experimentation, and death by starvation or gassing.

Brainwashing - How Terrorists Control Minds

Facts

One of the main examples of brainwashing being used in the modern era is by terrorist organizations. Many people will assume this means Islamist extremists, such as Al Qaeda and ISIS, but in actual fact, terrorists exist across the political spectrum. Violent terrorists might be motivated by their religious beliefs or strong political views originating from either the right or the left of the spectrum. What all of these diverse organizations share, however, is their use of brainwashing tactics to recruit and retain followers.

The power of such brainwashing cannot be overestimated. Countries from across the Western world are losing their young people to terrorists operating in the Middle East. How are such foreign organizations able to appeal so strongly? By using deliberate, carefully controlled brainwashing processes.

One particular aspect unique to the modern world of brainwashing is the terrorists' use of the Internet to support their aims and ideologies. Traditionally, brainwashing often had to occur in a physical context of close proximity, such as in a cult headquarters or some place similar. Thanks to the Internet, terror organizations are able to reach out and make contact with people, regardless of where in the world they live. The high-definition propaganda videos released by organizations are another tool in the new, high-tech world of brainwashing and indoctrination.

Although the modern world of terrorist related brainwashing features aspects never before seen, it also makes use of the tried-and-tested indoctrination methodologies that have been around for many years. The principles behind brainwashing are the same as they have ever been—the terrorist organizations are just applying them in technologically innovative ways.

The severity of this problem cannot be overestimated. Thanks to the untraceable reach of terrorist organizations through the Internet, no country or family is safe from the potential brainwashing that tragically occurs so frequently. This can involve young people with their whole lives ahead of them forsaking their familiar world to travel and die in a foreign war. It can also inspire mentally deranged individuals to perform "lone wolf" attacks on their own communities and nations.

Insights & Links to Dark Psychology

The modern use of brainwashing methods conducted through the Internet provides an application of classic principles updated for the modern world. Finding vulnerable victims is perhaps easier than ever before for those who wish to indoctrinate others. Thanks to the social norm of young people sharing their lives online, it is easy for almost anyone, no matter who they are or what intentions they have, to track down a target that will be susceptible to terror's insidious influence.

Thanks to the work of undercover journalists conducting sting operations, we have unparalleled insight into the current state of affairs regarding the brainwashing tactics used by terror organizations. After a victim has been identified, they will typically be assigned to one member of the terror group who it is felt will be able to communicate with them in an effective and influential way.

In line with classic brainwashing principles, the newly assigned recruiter will begin to work on their target slowly and methodically. Anything objectionable that the terror group represents will be hidden from sight until the victim has displayed a lot of willingness and open mindedness regarding potentially polarizing concepts.

Many modern terror organizations use the tried-and-tested method of presenting their own ideology as a utopian solution to the specific personal woes of the target. Regardless of whether the terror organization happens to be promoting Islamic extremism or right-wing racism, their tactics are more or less the same. They like to push a narrative of a society that has gone wrong and their proposed solution as the one answer to fix it. Such convincing portrayals are aided by the video and image abilities of the Internet, which allow groups to put across a heavily biased version of life within their ideology.

Much like classic brainwashing, modern terrorist efforts leave a victim feeling as if they are lucky and fortunate to have come into contact with the terrorist organization. Countless examples exist of young people with a lot to live for who, after being in prolonged contact with a terrorist brainwasher, end up expressing feelings of thanks and blessings for "discovering" their new outlook on life.

It is a mistake to assume that modern terror groups and their brainwashing efforts are solely focused on the Internet. This is not the case. Terrorists and other ideological extremists see the Internet as one tool among many they can use. The end goal of most groups is still to make physical contact with the individual and make them an offline part of their world as well. It is often when the victim moves into offline contact with the group that the severity of the brainwashing increases rapidly.

Modern terror groups are often aware that the utopian vision they have painted online will be rapidly exposed as patently false once the recruit spends some time among the group in person. For this reason, such groups are often quick to pressure the victim into establishing roots in the new world that they have chosen. This often involves marrying another member of the organization. Forming such close bonds to the group's offline activities helps to keep recruits enslaved, even after the utopian ideal is exposed as myth.

Rasputin - Black Magic or Dark Psychology?

Facts

No series of case studies on dark psychology would be complete without an examination of Rasputin and all that the infamous "mad monk" represents. Rasputin is an interesting figure as the type of dark psychological power he wielded echoed far into the future and inspired many aspects of charismatic influencers that appeared later on.

Who exactly was Rasputin? He was a spiritual figure who was able to gain influence over the ruling Russian elite of his era. Rasputin managed to project an intoxicating mix of piousness and sensuality that appealed to almost any side of a person Rasputin needed it to. Those who were inclined to be influenced by religion were easily impressed by the monk's apparent powers of healing. Those who preferred the sensual pleasures of the world found much to admire in Rasputin's character in that regard also. Perhaps the most devastatingly influential aspect of Rasputin's character was his ability to be both a devil and angel at the same time.

Many aspects of Rasputin's dark psychological influence can also be found in subsequent users of hypnosis. Rasputin is one of the earliest and most infamous figures who was able to induce something similar to a trancelike state of suggestibility in the minds and souls of his victims.

So what exactly were the "hypnotic" and "healing" powers Rasputin was rumored to have?

It was said that Rasputin was able to induce deep feelings of calm, ease, and relaxation in his victims. He was a forerunner to modern faith healers in many ways. Stories of his abilities to ease the aches and pains of the Russian nobility added to his mystique and the amount of influence he was able to have on almost everyone around him.

Rasputin also relates to many of the ideas found in the area of covert emotional manipulation. One of the reasons that the impact of Rasputin was so great and notorious was that he never seemed to be attempting to control his victims. Instead, it simply came across that he had some kind of inexplicable "power" and "aura" that people succumbed to. You will likely recognize these feelings as hallmarks of what we term "covert emotional manipulation" in the modern context.

Insights & Links to Dark Psychology

The case study of Rasputin is relevant for students of charismatic influence. In the modern context, many dark psychological manipulators are able to attract followers, due to the perception that they possess some kind of special or secret knowledge.

This principle was even more effective in the time of Rasputin. The world was less rational and science was far less developed. This gave greater credence to the perception of Rasputin as divine and mystically powerful. Students of dark psychology will be easily able to draw parallels between the power of this supernatural portrayal and similar charismatic leaders of the modern world who feign spirituality as a way of gaining influence and control.

The link between dark psychological power and sexual expression is also clear with Rasputin. Like countless others throughout history, he leveraged his dark psychological influence into a life of promiscuity and decadent indulgence. It is no coincidence that cult leaders across the world are often found enjoying their choice of followers, physically speaking. Rasputin is an infamous illustration of this principle, but he is by no means the first person to put it into practice.

The CIA Wants You To Kill People - MKUltra

Facts

The fact that this case study even exists is shocking. When we talk about MKUltra, what is it we are discussing? No less than the CIA's own prolonged and intense attempts to understand and develop mind-control techniques. This may well sound like the ramblings of a paranoid individual wearing a tinfoil hat, but it is anything but. Conduct your own research into MKUltra and you will see that the program was very real and very severe. By learning lessons from it we are able to see that even the most "civilized" nations recognize the power of brainwashing and attempt to use it for their own ends.

If the idea of a secret CIA program into mind control is hard to believe, then the details of the program are even more so. The CIA attempted to develop, test, and understand a wide range of mind-control techniques, including those that are purely physical, such as sleep deprivation, those that are psychological, such as identity erasing, and those that are pharmaceutical, such as "truth serums" and other drugs.

At least a research program of this type would have been carried out in the most proper and ethical way possible, right? Wrong. The program was totally illegal and unethical. How unethical? The administration of LSD and other substances to unwitting and unknowing US citizens was a hallmark of the program.

Some of the unproven aspects of the MKUltra program are the most disturbing of all. A theory exists which states that the CIA was able to hypnotically lead a man, Sirhan Sirhan, into assassinating a member of the Kennedy family. Credible witnesses, including psychologists, state that Sirhan was clearly operating under some kind of hypnotic influence during the murder itself and the subsequent trial phase. Sirhan has stated he has no recollection of anything that happened and cannot remember making statements he is on record as having made.

Insights & Links to Dark Psychology

The CIA's use of mind control techniques and research into their effectiveness has helped to pave the way for far more legitimate modern methods of influence. For example, MKUltra made pioneering use of combining drugs and psychological techniques to exert an influence on a target. Some modern psychologists are able to use this combination in a more positive way to treat psychological disorders, rather than only to manipulate and control.

Interestingly, MKUltra also shines light upon how Machiavellian tactics of political influence are alive and well even in modern-day America. The USA often portrays itself as a very ethical country that is not prepared to compromise on its values of freedom and equality. What MKUltra actually demonstrates is that the CIA is willing to take the Machiavellian approach of doing one thing publicly and another thing privately. When the CIA determined it was in its own interests to do so, it was willing to test dangerous psychedelic drugs on American citizens without their consent or understanding.

If the aspects of Sirhan Sirhan's involvement in MKUltra are ever verified, then terrifying possibilities become apparent. Such proof would verify, beyond a shadow of a doubt, that hypnotism can be used to directly influence someone to carry out an assassination. Some modern-day attempts at verifying these methods, or disproving them, have already been made. Modern-day hypnotist Derren Brown claims to have replicated the influence of MKUltra, but this claim may be down to some other form of illusion on behalf of Brown.

The Psychological Secrets of Con Artists

Facts

The fact that "Con Artists" are known by the second part of their title is a testament to the level of dark psychological skill they possess. Modern psychological researchers often express a deep level of surprise that many con artists have historically operated according to principles of influence that have only recently been proved by modern science. There is a clear indication that many of history's most infamous con artists have been dark psychological influencers with a mastery of principles the modern world is only just beginning to grasp.

Have you ever heard of a Ponzi scheme? The name is taken from a man, Charles Ponzi, who was able to conduct a large scale fraudulent investment scheme. One of the most striking features of this original Ponzi scheme is Charles's willingness to use the power of projection and portrayal of his own confidence to get out of sticky situations. For example, Charles once had a group of angry investors arrive at his place of business. Rather than panicking, as many people would, Charles was able to remain calm and collected and placate the mob through his tranquil, inspiring demeanor.

Faith healers share some similarities with Charles Ponzi insofar as they prey on their victims' vulnerability to serve their own aims. Whereas Ponzi made use of his victims' desperation for money and financial success, faith healers take the more deplorable approach of exploiting someone's sickness and misery, coupled with their victim's desire for a religious experience, to manipulate them.

The ramifications of encountering a fraudulent faith healer can be very serious indeed. Many stories exist of people who have believed they have been healed as a result of contact with a faith healer. As a result of this apparent healing they stop taking medication or do something else medically risky as a display of trust and belief. Sadly, people have died from taking these risks.

Another infamous con artist from the pages of history is Gregor MacGregor. He is only of the earliest known examples of someone selling things that don't exist to rich people. If you have ever heard the stories of con artists selling landmarks like the Eiffel Tower or Brooklyn Bridge to naive folks with wealth, Gregor MacGregor is the Godfather of this type of con.

MacGregor operated by insisting he was nobility from a group of islands that did not exist. He would recruit people with wealth to fund expeditions to these islands, knowing full well they weren't there. This is interesting, but how exactly is it a valuable case study in dark psychology?

The reason there is so much interest in MacGregor is that he was so convincing to his victims, and knew how to work their egos and psyches to a detailed and thorough extent, that even after they had attempted to visit nonexistent islands, they defended MacGregor in the press! This is indicative of MacGregor's advanced-level covert manipulation abilities.

Insights & Links to Dark Psychology

There are many lessons on dark psychology to be learned from the con artists. Their ability to psychologically influence other people is such that even modern psychological researchers have expressed amazement at the extent to which con men made use of modern psychological findings before they were confirmed by science.

The case of Ponzi shows the importance of finding a victim with a vulnerability, ruthlessly exploiting that vulnerability, and doing so in a way that betrays no doubt or hesitation whatsoever. Ponzi is a textbook example of how to increase the likelihood of a fraud working out by simply coming across as confident, in control, and unworried at all times. Ponzi is also illustrative of the concept that the best con artists are able to keep their scams going for decades without being exposed.

Faith healers offer an insight into the suggestibility of the minds of victims. These healers are convincing to the extent that their victims made detrimental medical decisions and even died as a result. Faith healers also demonstrate why so many people are susceptible to the influence of charismatic religious cults. When a strong spiritual belief is mixed with a real world need, such as the need to find relief from an ailment, people can be driven to extreme measures.

Finally, MacGregor offers an amusing insight into the power of using people's own egos against them. Despite the fact that his wealthy investors had been exploited financially, had their time wasted, and been made to look stupid in the process, they still chose to publicly defend MacGregor!

What is the dark psychological lesson we can take from this? If a victim is found who has high status and a high opinion of themselves, they are unlikely to admit they have been tricked or conned. They will not even admit the true state of events within their own mind! Interestingly, this is an example of how someone's narcissism can be used against them!

Heavenly Psychopaths - A Soldier's Secrets

Facts

Since the term "psychopath" became prevalent in the field of psychology, and also in the popular imagination, it has been associated with negativity. One of the earliest high-profile psychologists, Bowlby, linked the concept to a deprivation of maternal attention during childhood and stated that such people would usually grow up to be delinquent criminals who were a burden on society.

Andy McNab is an intriguing example of someone with psychopathic traits who many would see as a "good psychopath" if such a thing exists. McNab was abandoned as a baby and fell into a life of petty crime before joining the army as a young man. He went on to rise up through the ranks and join Britain's elite SAS special forces unit. Since retiring from the world of the armed forces McNab has become a successful author, playwright, and entrepreneur.

Dr. Dutton is a leading British psychological researcher. He collaborated on a book with McNab that explored the idea that psychopathic traits were actually useful in some situations. This concept is somewhat revolutionary as it explores the positive implications and advantages of an aspect of dark psychology that is usually maligned extensively.

Dutton and McNab were able to identify a few fields in which they felt the dark psychological traits bestowed by psychopathy would actually lead to a practical advantage. One example is anyone who has to respond to an emergency crisis. Most regular people are unlikely to perform as well as psychopaths. This is due to the presence of fear in their mind causing doubt and hesitation in their action. McNab was able to explain that, for a psychopath, it is possible to dial down the fear response at will. This allows psychopaths to operate calmly amid situations that would be too overwhelming for most people to handle.

High-risk financial fields such as hedge fund management are another area that McNab and Dutton identified as being suitable for psychopaths. One feature of psychopathy is impulsivity, and this allows for risky decisions to be made with little hesitation or fear. In the wrong context, this can lead to murders being carried out without a second thought, but in the right context, this can lead to millions being made on the financial markets.

Insights & Links to Dark Psychology

Many dark psychological insights can be gleaned from the work of McNab and Dutton. Their collaboration is extremely beneficial to the world of dark psychology as it combines the theoretical knowledge of a researcher with the practical experience and firsthand anecdotes of an actual psychopath who has used their traits to get ahead in the world in more than one field.

This suggests that the way that the dark trait of psychopathy manifests in any given individual is largely dependent on the circumstances in which they find themselves. If someone is born with psychopathy and also lacks advantages and opportunities, they are liable to become a dangerous person, such as Ted Bundy. If a psychopath is able to channel their urges into a career that is suitable for them, then they are more likely to become a conventional success in life, such as Andy McNab.

How a Cocaine Sniffing Murder Suspect Created NLP

Facts

In an earlier section of this book we explored the concept of hypnotism as something that exists and can be used by practitioners of dark psychology to influence those around them. NLP, or neurolinguistic programming, is one of the main techniques that hypnotists use to influence others. The technique is fascinating and worth knowing about. A case study of one of its co-creators, Richard Bandler, offers deep insight into the concept of hypnotic influence and other areas of dark psychology.

Richard Bandler is a controversial character and a textbook example of how users of dark psychology are able to portray one image of their life when the actual truth may be something entirely different. Let's explore this dichotomy.

On one hand, Richard Bandler claims a wide range of impressive therapeutic achievements, such as using his own methods to no longer need a wheelchair and curing patients such as schizophrenics with unconventional and innovative techniques that were dismissed out of hand by the world of mainstream psychology. Because of these achievements, many people who do not know much about Bandler expect him to be a mild-mannered, grandfatherly type who lives and breathes positivity.

The actual truth about Bandler is a lot more complex than one would first expect. He grew up in abusive environments in which he was physically attacked by a series of different adult males. He also lives in violation of many of the things he often claims his techniques are able to fix in a person's life.

For example, Bandler claims his NLP and other similar techniques he has worked on are able to cure a person of the bad and unhealthy habits that plague their life. Despite this, Bandler smoked cigarettes for many years. Cigarettes were far from his only vice. Bandler is a publicly admitted past user of cocaine, an interesting trait for a well-known public hypnotist.

Perhaps the darkest and most intriguing incident from Bandler's background is the murder trial he faced. What is undisputed is that a woman was shot using Bandler's gun. Bandler was cleared of the crime and insists that his cocaine dealer used his gun to carry out the killing. When reminiscing about the incident, Bandler is more likely to comment on the time it took for the jury to clear him than the gravity and potential severity of the incident itself.

Bandler's use of narcotics is interesting as he is not the only high-profile figure within the field of psychology to do so. Sigmund Freud, the originator of modern psychoanalysis, was actually an avid cocaine user and insisted it was suitable for therapeutic use. These two men are textbook examples of how pioneers in the field of dark psychology are unlikely to be restrained by the rules of society and instead determine what is and is not acceptable for their own lives.

Insights & Links to Dark Psychology

Many insights into the world of dark psychology in general, and hypnotism in particular, can be taken from the case study of Richard Bandler. Perhaps the most striking aspect of his character and life is his ability to inspire totally different reactions in people. Some people are extremely dedicated to him and volunteer large amounts of their own time and money to spend time around him. Others view him as one of the most dangerous people in the world—a drug user mixed up in murder who happens to possess some of the strongest powers of influence ever witnessed.

One thing that is certain about Richard Bandler is he is the master of the NLP concept of a reframe. When he is asked about his use of cocaine he is quick to point out that he was more addicted to foods like candy and peanuts and insists they were actually worse for his health! Taken at first glance, this insistence shows how Bandler is able to make a serious situation into a lighthearted, even rational situation by the use of a comparative reframe.

Dig deeper, however, and you will realize that Bandler's cocaine dealer killed someone, using Bandler's gun, and Bandler stood trial for this murder. Despite the severity of this situation and the fact it involved a loss of human life, Bandler is able to compare cocaine to peanuts.

The story of Bandler is also a prime example of how skilled hypnotists, and users of NLP, are able to control the selective focus of the person they are manipulating. Bandler often manages to express his disdain for questions about his personal life, insisting that he has helped thousands of people over the years and this is largely ignored in favor of his personal vices. This argument also seems reasonable at first glance, but it loses its appeal once the fact of Bandler's smoking, drug use, and ill-tempered parting of ways with his NLP co-creator are remembered.

Another area of dark psychology that Bandler is perhaps the master of is undetected mind control. Countless examples exist of Bandler's patients who claim to have had life-changing experiences interacting with him that they don't understand, don't remember, and can't explain. To have such a profound influence on people without giving away any idea whatsoever of what's actually taken place is a signature feature of undetected mind control. Anyone who doubts the power, or existence, of this technique needs only to consider the power of Bandler and the endless testimonies that tell tales of his mastery.

Exposing the Cult Control Methods

Facts

In the earlier chapters of this book we explored how cults use brainwashing techniques in general to attract new members. We will now look at some case studies of specific cults and the techniques they use to gain insight into the ways brainwashing is applied to suit the agenda of a particular group.

The Ku Klux Klan, or KKK, is a secretive white supremacist organization that is largely underground following its prominence in earlier decades. Recruiters for the KKK tend to use classic brainwashing methodology adopted for their own aims and objectives. By looking at their usage of these techniques we can see how the process can be adapted to fit a bespoke agenda.

Like all brainwashing, the KKK's begins by finding a suitable target to brainwash. This will often be a young white male who is down on his luck. Some common targets for the group include men who have recently lost their jobs or experienced some other type of misfortune.

The KKK recruiter will initially begin by avoiding any mention of the group. They will simply reach out to the target under the guise of a concerned friend and neighbor who wants to help out in a time of need. Slowly, the KKK recruiter will explore the grievances that their target has and begin to link these to other races. So if the recruit had lost their job, for example, the recruiter would slowly begin to make sure the recruit linked this to the presence of other races in America.

Over time, the KKK recruiter will begin to explore overtly racist ideas with the recruit, but always cloaked with the cover of "promoting white Brotherhood" and "standing up for our own people." Depending on how the recruit responds to such concepts, and whether the recruiter feels they will be a suitable and trusted member of the Klan, they may gradually receive an invitation to attend some Klan events, meet other members and find out if the organization is something that is right for them. These earliest exposures are likely to be low-key, social events such as BBQs. This lures in the new recruit before they ever see something as extreme as a cross-burning ceremony.

The KKK recruitment process is a clear example of how cults and extremist political groups often are similar in their nature and the way they use brainwashing to attract new recruits. The People's Temple in Jonestown was another example of how cults often have a mystical dimension that attracts followers and causes them to carry out extreme acts.

Jim Jones was a charismatic cult leader who managed to amass land, power, and influence to a terrifying extent. Just as the KKK blurs the lines between a cult, political group and terrorist organization, Jonestown was a group that featured a mixture of extreme left-wing politics, messianic obedience to Jones, and vague spiritual notions such as suicide and reincarnation.

The methods of Jim Jones are yet another testament to the power of graduality in the brainwashing process. Jones would initially gain the interest of potential recruiters by exploring what seemed like rational political ideas and judging their support for alternative concepts, such as the Soviet system. Initiates to the organization slowly surrendered their sanity and freedom, leading up to the shocking final act in the group's demise.

Jonestown ended in a way that is tragically common to cults—mass suicide. After imploring his followers to carry out a political assassination, Jones led his organization in a mass suicide. Mothers administered poisoned Kool-Aid to their babies and Jones himself put a bullet through his brain. Jonestown is a clear warning of the extreme danger that dark psychology represents. When paranoid, charismatic leaders are granted autonomy and control over others, and this is mixed with a high level of isolation from wider society, it can lead to utterly unimaginable outcomes, such as the mass poisoning of babies.

One of the most shocking and famous examples of the power of isolation to influence a person to carry out the aims of a group is the case of Patty Hearst. Hearst grew up in a famous and respected family before being kidnapped by a cultish political fringe group known as the SLA.

The kidnapping and subsequent events surrounding Hearst are testimony to the methods of brainwashing in action. During the kidnapping itself, she was violently attacked. After being taken to the headquarters of the SLA she was kept in total isolation, blindfolded, in a closet. This extreme isolation and sensory deprivation continued for a period of time until the SLA began to inform Hearst that she would possibly be killed.

Gradually, the group began to allow Hearst to join in with political discussions and she was eventually given the choice of joining the group. Only after confirming this was her choice was she allowed to remove her blindfold and lay eyes upon her captors. After her "allegiance" was declared, Hearst began to suffer extreme narcotic and sexual torture in the form of rape and drug use.

The eventual outcome of this extreme physical and political brainwashing was the previously respected and respectable Hearst participating in a range of crimes on behalf of the SLA, including documented bank robberies in which she wielded a machine gun and made violent threats toward the public.

One of the most interesting aspects of the Hearst case is the empirical evidence of brainwashing's impact that became available following her eventual arrest. Psychiatrists were able to conclusively show that, following the brainwashing process, Hearst's IQ had dropped and this amounted to a state in which she was a "zombie." This impact was so extreme that Hearst had her sentence commuted and eventually received a full Presidential pardon.

Insights & Links to Dark Psychology

The brainwashing techniques of these extremist cults offer an unparalleled glimpse into the use and impact of dark psychology.

The KKK case study illustrates how brainwashing recruiters are able to skillfully find a point of weakness in a victim's life and mercilessly exploit this to bend the victim to the group's will. Their methods show how the particular ideological or political motivation behind brainwashing is rarely important—a skilled recruiter will be able to bend a vulnerable victim to almost any perspective, given enough time and patience.

Jonestown shows how isolation can lead to utter insanity. Just as modern brainwashers such as

ISIS end up isolating people to the point they take their own life for a political cause, Jonestown established the blueprint for this very practice. The eventual end game of Jim Jones shows how for controlling cult leaders, the ultimate expression of their power and influence is often the mass deaths of others.

The case of Patty Hearst and the SLA shows how brainwashing can take a more forceful and rapid path than the traditional route of graduality. It is testament to the power of Stockholm Syndrome that Hearst seemed to "willingly" act according to the interests of her captors, even when she was no longer physically restrained. This is a clear sign that the psychological shackles imposed by a brainwasher are far more powerful than any physical chains could ever be.

Conclusion: Light At The End Of The Tunnel?

What We've Learned

You now have a map of the most dangerous minds to ever have existed.

You know the principles that underpin the world of dark psychology. You know how these principles are applied and modified to different situations. You are able to recognize the traits of the people most likely to be seeking to exert their dark psychological powers over you.

Clear case studies have offered insight into the outer limits of dark psychology and the way it has been applied throughout human history.

Shield or Sword?

Every reader of this book will have had a slightly different experience.

Did you get the sense of learning powerful defensive tactics and ideas you could use to protect yourself and your loved ones from the evil of the world?

Or was your experience a little…darker? A little more exciting? Perhaps you feel you now have a valuable secret weapon you can use to get ahead in the world.

Whatever your experience has been, you know now the reality of life. There is no going back.

This book can be considered a rulebook for the true game of life.

Whichever way you want to play is entirely up to you.

Printed in Great Britain
by Amazon